GUIDE TO THE
MANAGEMENT
GURUS

GUIDE TO THE MANAGEMENT GURUS

SHORTCUTS TO THE IDEAS OF LEADING MANAGEMENT THINKERS

CAROL KENNEDY

BUSINESS BOOKS LIMITED

The right of Carol Kennedy to be identified as the author of this work
has been asserted by her in accordance with the Copyright, Designs
and Patents Act 1988

First published in 1991 in Great Britain by
Business Books Limited
An imprint of Random Century Limited
20 Vauxhall Bridge Road, London SW1V 2SA

Random Century Australia (Pty) Limited
20 Alfred Street, Milsons Point, Sydney
New South Wales 2061, Australia

Random Century New Zealand Limited
9–11 Rothwell Avenue, Albany, Glenfield
Auckland 10, New Zealand

Random Century South Africa (Pty) Limited
PO Box 337, Bergvlei, South Africa

Set in Bembo by 🅰 Tek Art Limited
Addiscombe, Croydon, Surrey

Printed and bound in Great Britain by
Mackays of Chatham PLC, Chatham, Kent

British Library Cataloguing in Publication Data
A catalogue record for this book is available from the British Library

ISBN 0–09–174810–0
ISBN 0–7126–4347–8 (Pbk bookclub only)

CONTENTS

INTRODUCTION

The Age of the Guru

There is a limit to the number of original ideas in any field of human activity, and management is no exception. After all, it is said that there are no more than half a dozen basic plots throughout the whole world of fiction and drama. Some of the most enduring themes of management were conceived centuries before commercial or industrial management was born – let alone the concept of the management guru with his or her prescriptives for performance.

Machiavelli's *The Prince*, written at the height of Renaissance Florence, is still a classic text on leadership and the uses of power (and inspired a popular management book of the 1960s by Antony Jay). The translator of its best-selling Penguin edition, George Bull, says *The Prince*'s precepts are 'perfectly applicable to the actions of captains of industry or budding entrepreneurs,' citing as just one example Machiavelli's advice that when a ruler seizes a state (or a new chief executive moves into a company), he must do the hardest things first. 'The new ruler must determine all the injuries that he will need to inflict. He must inflict them once and for all, and not have to renew them every day. In that way he will be able to set men's minds at rest, and win them over to him when he confers benefits.' Every takeover king has instinctively practised that.

Further back in history, the basic human responses to work and responsibility were articulated by Plato and Aristotle in their differing views of man; the one believing authoritarian direction was needed if anything of value was to be accomplished, the other that man as a 'social' or 'political' animal required a sense of participation in his own destiny. In the 1960s Douglas McGregor dressed up the concepts with sociological research into industrial practice and presented them as Theory X and Theory Y – authoritarian versus democratic management. It became one of the great management theories of the decade.

Digging even deeper into antiquity, management writers have adapted the wisdom of Taoism to the modern executive office. There is even a book on management in Shakespeare and jokey exercises on Genghis Khan and Attila the Hun as business tacticians. No doubt the Roman emperors will one day yield a book on leadership strategy.

Variations on ideas, of course, are infinite – or can be made to seem so. It is this which accounts for the vast numbers of management books that pour annually from publishing houses on both sides of the Atlantic, and for the lucrative lecture circuits and all the paraphernalia of commercially packaged wisdom that bring handsome incomes – indeed, millionaire status – to the leading management gurus.

The management guru whose precepts are bought as the key to success is essentially a phenomenon of the last 30 to 40 years. Before World War II, when, as Peter Drucker has recalled, 'all the books on management filled no more than a modest shelf' – perhaps 70 in all languages except Japanese – the thinkers on management who won the admiration of their peers could be numbered on the fingers of one hand.

Several were career businessmen whose management wisdom was distilled into books long after they had learned it on the job; notably Alfred P. Sloan of General Motors, who built the world's largest corporation out of a medium-sized, ailing automobile manufacturer, and Chester Barnard of AT&T, who wrote what remained for many years the definitive text on the functions of the executive. Sloan's memoirs, *My Life With General Motors*, is still revered, 30 years after publication and some 65 years after the events it chronicled, as the classic exposition of how to create a great business enterprise by applying the principles of total marketing and decentralization.

In Britain, the lone management theorist in the 1930s was Lyndall Urwick, who had been converted to 'scientific management' as an officer in the Flanders trenches by reading the works of Frederick W. Taylor, the progenitor of time and motion study. In 1934 Urwick set up Britain's first management consultancy, Urwick Orr and Partners.

Others who worked away in the interwar years, reacting against Taylor's mechanistic approach by studying the human element in organizations and the springs of motivation, including Elton Mayo with his experiments at Western Electric's Hawthorne plant in Chicago (a forcing house for later gurus), did not publish their findings until the 1950s or 1960s. Then, backed by distinguished academic appointments in North American universities, they became almost instant gurus.

Curiously, the phenomenon is virtually absent from Japan and the 'tiger' economies of the Pacific Rim. These appear to generate world-beating success in business without benefit of home-grown gurus, unless one counts the heads of Honda, Sony and Matsushita, who have achieved a certain guru status through the way they run their companies. (Japan's one great obeisance to management gurus remains its homage to America's W. Edwards Deming and Joseph Juran, who converted the Japanese in the 1950s to the principles of quality control.) Since the word 'guru' (a Sanskrit derivation meaning weighty and extended to mean a Hindu priest), originated in the East, one may ask why Eastern businesses have been able to manage pretty well without them. The inescapable conclusion is that in the West everything has to be marketed before it is taken seriously – and that goes for the whole management improvement business. Not surprisingly, a number of leading US academics who enjoy high guru status dislike being tagged with the word, though nearly all have highly commercial consultancies and are no strangers to marketing their own skills.

How are gurus born or created? Many a management writer and professor of business studies has laboured towards the elusive goal without ever coming close to it, while others seem to be elevated to guru status without even trying. You can be a highly successful author, invent a genre of books like Kenneth Blanchard's *The One-Minute Manager*, and still not approach gurudom, however much in demand you are on the lecture or after-dinner circuit.

You can be a captain of industry with a brilliant track record at turning companies around and a gift for the best-selling memoir, like Sir John Harvey-Jones, Lee Iacocca or Harold Geneen, and spend a lucrative retirement passing on high-priced pearls of wisdom to business or TV audiences – yet still not rank as a true guru.

You can make a career out of futurology like Alvin Toffler and John Naisbitt in the US, or Francis Kinsman in the UK, and be quoted for years on phrases like 'Future Shock,' 'The Third Wave' or 'Megatrends' – yet ultimately fail the guru test. (Gurus have to be measured against the hard problems of here and now: Charles Handy's explorations of the future are solidly rooted in present dilemmas, and besides, he won his spurs as an expert on business organizations.)

You can beaver away for years in university or business school or polytechnic back offices, producing brilliant theses and papers that might eventually become the only work of their kind on, say, long-range planning in the electronics industry, or the development of an Asian management style. In the past that might have brought guru status in time, starting with a small circle of fellow-academics and filtering into the business world; today's harsh demands of media and marketing combine to make it very difficult for the quiet thinker or teacher to achieve gurudom.

The three leading gurus in the world today are generally acknowledged to be Peter Drucker, Tom Peters and Michael Porter. The first is in his eighties and, by virtue of his long reputation and productivity over the years, immune to the pressures of the video age, though he pursues an active international round of seminars. The others are in their forties and – though Porter is a Harvard academic – they have grown up with telecommunications, marketing hype and the need to add a gloss of show-business to selling their wares.

Watch Tom Peters (he and Porter vie with each other for the highest lecture fees in the business) pacing the platform, pouring megawatts of energy into his exposition, his shirt dark with sweat after only a few minutes. He is more an evangelist of business ideas than a teacher; he entertains and inspires as well as informs. Porter is somewhat lower key in style but engages his audience with humour and painlessly lures them into dense intellectual concepts with brilliantly packaged analytic models and flip-charts.

Packaging, indeed, is half the art, or even more, of becoming a guru in the 1990s. As *Business Week* reported in the summer of 1990, some academics and consultants in the US regard Porter's concepts on competitive strategy as gimmicky, but nearly all acknowledge that he is 'a master at packaging and marketing ideas.' Porter himself talks about the importance of 'the Michael Porter brand', and this is emphatically the trend today, to become as identified with a business theory as Porter is with competitive strategy and competitive advantage. The underlying truths may be as old as trading itself, but Porter has branded them, and as such they are supremely saleable. By mid-1990, *Business Week* reported, his royalties on four books, beginning with *Competitive Strategy* in 1980, had brought him over $2m.

Gurudom can start with one stunningly successful book, a book that every executive must be seen with. The prime example here is, of course, Peters' and Waterman's *In Search of Excellence* – still reprinting in its original format ten years after first publication, despite the fact that two-thirds of its 'excellent' companies have since faded from glory and that Peters himself opened his second book, *Thriving on Chaos*, with the cheeky statement: 'There are no excellent companies.'

Of the two authors, however, only Peters has chosen to haul himself up to the top rung of international gurus; his temperamentally opposite co-author Bob Waterman, a quiet, reflective Californian, prefers a less stressful, time-pressured existence. Waterman's first solo book, *The*

Renewal Factor, is regarded by some management teachers as a far deeper, more intellectually rigorous work than Peters' best-selling *Thriving on Chaos*, but it is Peters who commands the global 'branding' factor and the huge fees that go with it.

Of course branding, packaging and a flair for show-business are only part of the answer. What marks out the real guru – the one who will be read in business schools and boardrooms – from the business hero turned media celebrity, or the author who hits on a jokey formula like the *One-Minute Manager* or the business strategy of Genghis Khan, is the ability to generate original, durable thinking on the hard matter of managing people and resources.

All the gurus whose ideas are summarized in this book (and no summaries can do full justice to a lifetime of thinking: their key books should be read) meet this requirement, even out-of-date theorists like F.W. Taylor and Max Weber. Their ideas were not only important in their time; they have been adapted and built on for generations, even if they have been partly destroyed in order to use the bricks again. And in some quarters they have not been wholly destroyed: Robert Waterman muses that many more managers are Taylorists at heart than would ever admit it.

Gurus broadly divide into those with one Big Idea – Edward de Bono's lateral thinking is a perfect example, out of which he has spun a sparkling web of books, international seminars and blue-chip consultancy – and those, like Peter Drucker and Charles Handy, whose fizzing intellects spray ideas in all directions; about the future of work and society, new designs for organizations, geopolitical shifts and managing change. Michael Porter's emphasis on competitive strategy puts him basically in the first category (a Big Idea can have endless spin-offs), while Tom Peters shows signs of developing into a multi-ideas guru.

All have one thing in common: they build on each other's ideas and on their own. There is nothing remotely discreditable or plagiaristic in this: it is only what historians and philosophers have done down the ages. The Californian professor of management William Ouchi had a tremendous success with his 1981 book *Theory Z*, which used the terminology of McGregor's Theory X and Theory Y, going a step beyond Theory Y to describe, with case studies, the kind of consensus-seeking management which has succeeded so brilliantly in Japan. McGregor himself had begun to formulate a Theory Z, but did not have time to develop it in depth before he died. Richard Pascale, in *Managing on the Edge*, says McGregor's last theory was quickly forgotten, and it was reborn independently as the archetype of Japanese business practice.

Another typical piece of guru language – gurus can be identified by their ability to invent terms that go into the management vocabulary, like Theory X, the psychological contract or lateral thinking – that has gone through many retreads is 'adhocracy.' The term, meaning, roughly, the opposite of bureaucracy, a flexible sort of task force that crosses the frontiers within organizations, first surfaced in Warren Bennis' *The Temporary Society* in 1968, gained wider currency in Alvin Toffler's *Future Shock* in 1970, emerged independently in Henry Mintzberg's *The Structuring of Organizations* in 1979 and, most recently, formed the subject of an entire short book by Robert Waterman. Charles Handy has also explored the implications of the term. 'We all build on each other's work,' smiled Waterman when asked about the genesis of his title.

Everybody, for two generations of gurudom, has drawn somewhere on Drucker, that monumental quarry of management wisdom and original thought. Even Theories X and Y, as McGregor acknowledged, synthesized the ideas of others, including some which Drucker had presented in three early books – *Concept of the Corporation*, *The New Society*, and *The Practice of Management*. Peters and Waterman, too, said that much of what they discovered in identifying their principles of excellence had first been aired by Drucker 30 years before.

There are few great themes of management, just as there are few great plots in fiction. Probably the richest vein, and the one that has attracted most theorists over the years, involves the human side of management, understanding what motivates men and women to work and to strive for better performance. Frederick Taylor thought that efficiency was all, and that it could be measured and mastered by a stopwatch; later gurus tackled more complex, deeper themes.

The first area to be explored in management writing, by the French mining manager Henri Fayol at the turn of the century, was the function of management itself; still a fertile field as the late 20th century continues to be obsessed with how to manage change and discontinuity. Another early and long-lived theme is organizational theory, including hierarchies and the need or otherwise for them, and the now fashionable 'flatter management structures' which are supposed to 'empower' the employee farther down the line. 'Empowerment' is a new subdivision of this genre (or maybe a new word for an old concept) and the formidable Rosabeth Moss Kanter, who edits the *Harvard Business Review* along with teaching, consultancy and writing influential books, has explored all that this implies for releasing the forces of change and innovation within organizations.

The search for better organizational performance is an almost inexhaustible field, with spin-offs ranging from strategy to marketing to company culture to the art of the mission statement. In Britain, the Strategic Management Centre set up by Ashridge Management College is breeding a stable of potential gurus in strategy and corporate missions, headed by Andrew Campbell and Michael Goold. If anything could hinder their progress to guru status it is probably their prolific output of books, and the changing permutations of authors. Gurus rarely come in pairs and even more rarely stay in pairs: Anthony Athos, who co-authored *The Art of Japanese Management* with Richard Pascale in 1981, has vanished from view, and Pascale took nine years before bursting into print again – most successfully – with *Managing on the Edge*. He is now firmly established as a solo guru of fast-growing influence.

Leadership is a field that has attracted surprisingly few gurus, perhaps because its mystique, like that of monarchy, is hard to expose to daylight; leadership, ultimately, may be in the eye of the beholder. The US leadership guru James McGregor Burns, a political scientist and active campaigner for President John F. Kennedy, described leadership as 'one of the most observed and least understood phenomena on earth.' Burns was the first to identify the distinction between 'transactional' and 'transformational' leadership, explaining that the first is a tacit agreement to exchange one benefit for another (ie, jobs for votes) while a leader of the second type engages in a deeper relationship with his followers. 'The transforming leader looks for potential motives in followers, seeks to satisfy higher needs . . . .'

Why Burns has not become as famous in the field as Warren Bennis, who started out as an organizational theorist, is curious, but only one of many anomalies in what may be called the greater and lesser guru syndrome. Another US lesser guru of leadership, one with a steadily advancing reputation, is John Kotter, professor of organizational behaviour and human resource management at Harvard Business School. His study of senior management, *The General Managers* (1982) presented an impressive argument that many of the skills once thought to be needed only by top managers in an organization were increasingly needed lower down the line. His 1990 book *A Force For Change: How Leadership Differs from Management*, attempts to analyse the quality that, he contends, is essential to make change happen in organizations.

Lesser gurus may well progress in time to greater status, though it is hard to shine against established stars in a particular field. The duopoly of Harvard professor Christopher Bartlett and INSEAD professor Sumantra Ghoshal produced, in 1989, a book called *Managing Across Borders* that was of much more practical value to managers in multinationals than Kenichi Ohmae's later and more abstract work *The Borderless World*. Yet Ohmae has guru status, and his book, though undermined in its thesis that nationalism is on the wane by events in the Gulf, rides on a reputation created by *The Mind of the Strategist* and *Triad Power*.

Bartlett and Ghoshal delved into case studies as fascinating in their application to global-marketing companies as those on Japanese and US companies in *The Art of Japanese Management*. As the single market in Europe becomes a reality and a challenge, they too may find their hour as did

Pascale and Athos when US industrialists were running scared of the Japanese threat and desperate to learn how to defeat it. Timing is of the essence in achieving gurudom.

Timing; originality; forcefulness; a gift for self-promotion and perhaps above all else, the ability to encapsulate memorably what others immediately recognize as true – these are the marks of the modern management guru. Peters and Waterman created the first mass-selling management book – the one everyone needed to read – by packaging some fundamental truths in snappy slogans like 'stick to the knitting.' Beneath the glossy paintwork, however, was a solidly built motor that, while not entirely original in every part, would probably last as long as the heavy-duty classics of Chandler, Barnard and Mayo – indeed, was partly cannibalized from those very vehicles.

One thing is certain: in an age of incessant searching for a grail of business and personal success that recedes as surely as Gatsby's green light into the distance, of the making of management gurus there is no foreseeable end.

JOHN ADAIR

(b.1934)

Action-Centred Leadership : how Task, Team and Individual overlap

Pioneering British thinker in the theory and practice of leadership, and the first to occupy a chair in leadership studies in the UK (at the University of Surrey, 1979–1983).

Cambridge graduate Adair, whose quiet and business-like demeanour is belied by a colourful career including service in a Bedouin regiment under Glubb Pasha; working as a deckhand on an Arctic trawler, and lecturing at the Royal Military Academy, Sandhurst, has written more than 25 books on leadership and management development. He now works as an international management consultant and runs his own publishing company as well as maintaining his academic links with the University of Surrey.

Before his appointment to the leadership chair, Adair was visiting fellow at the Oxford Centre for Management Studies and assistant director of The Industrial Society, where he headed the leadership department.

Adair believes his contribution to management thinking is threefold. He can claim to have been the first to demonstrate that people can be trained for leadership as a transferable skill rather than a matter of inborn aptitude. Second, he has helped alter the concept of management to include the larger element of leadership, with which he associated the neighbouring skills of decision-making, communication, and ability to manage time. Finally, he has defined leadership in terms of three overlapping circles – Task, Team and Individual – distilled into his teaching concept, Action-Centred Learning (ACL).

Without undue modesty, Adair suggests that the ACL model is 'emerging in management studies, in effect, as something akin to Einstein's General Theory of Relativity.' It does, he maintains, 'identify the main forces at work in working groups and organisations, and it charts . . . their main interrelationships with a degree of predictive accuracy.'

ACL encompasses much of the teaching on individual human needs first charted by Abraham Maslow (qv) and Frederick Herzberg (qv). It was developed by Adair first at Sandhurst and later at The Industrial Society.

Adair's best-known books on leadership are *Effective Leadership*, *Not Bosses But Leaders* and *Great Leaders*, a study of leadership qualities in historical figures. He is concerned now to think out what the 'next family of concepts' will be for the mid-1990s, and he claims his 'mission' is to be 'in the forefront of long-term management thinking' and to integrate management concepts to better effect.

John Adair goes to etymological roots to explain the crucial difference between 'leading' and 'managing'. In an interview in *Director* magazine (November 1988), he explained it neatly:

Leadership is about a sense of direction. The word 'lead' comes from an Anglo-Saxon word, common to north European languages, which means a road, a way, the path of a ship at sea. It's knowing what the next step is . . . . Managing is a different image. It's from the Latin manus, a hand. It's handling a sword, a ship, a horse. It tends to be closely linked with the idea of machines. Managing had its origins in the 19th century with

2

engineers and accountants coming in to run entrepreneurial outfits. They tended to think of them as systems.

But there are valuable ingredients in the concept of management that are not present in leadership. Managing is very strong on the idea of controlling, particularly financial control, and administration. Leaders are not necessarily good at administration or managing resources.

What leaders are – or should be – good at, he elaborated in the same interview, is inspiring others. 'That's tied in with the leader's own enthusiasm and commitment and with the ability to communicate and share that enthusiasm with others and to enthuse them. It's not quite the same as motivation, which is something that's learned about in the business schools, a rather mechanical thing.

'And leadership is about teamwork, creating teams. Teams tend to have leaders, leaders tend to create teams.

'Finally, you can be appointed a manager, but you're not a leader until your appointment is "ratified" in the hearts and minds of those who work for you. There's got to be a degree of acceptance of you by followers that is not necessary if you're just holding an appointment.'

The ethos of the team is at the heart of Adair's leadership theories and his Action-Centred Learning model. He believes that working groups share three areas of common needs: the need to accomplish a common task, the need to be maintained as a cohesive social unit or team, and the sum of the group's individual needs. These form his overlapping 'three-circle model': failure in one area affects the other two. For example, failure to achieve the task (or lack of a task altogether) will both disrupt the sense of teamship and lower the level of individual satisfaction. The approach can best be understood by drawing three interlocking circles labelled Task, Team and Individual and placing a coin over any one of them. Segments of the other two are immediately blotted out. The overlapping circles, maintains Adair, illustrate 'the essential unity of leadership; a single action can be multi-functional in that it touches all areas.'

In a recent book entitled *Understanding Motivation* (1990),

Adair lists the functions of leadership as originally worked out at Sandhurst:

- Planning (seeking all available information: defining group tasks or goals; making a workable plan)
- Initiating (briefing the group; allocating tasks; setting group standards)
- Controlling (maintaining group standards; ensuring progress towards objectives; 'prodding' actions and decisions)
- Supporting (expressing acceptance of individual contributions; encouraging and disciplining; creating team spirit; relieving tension with humour; reconciling disagreements)
- Informing (clarifying task and plan; keeping group informed; receiving information from the group; summarizing ideas and suggestions)
- Evaluating (checking feasibility of ideas; testing consequences; evaluating group performance; helping group to evaluate itself)

The functions of leadership are a key element in Adair's integrated ACL theory, in which the three-circle model plays a central role without being the whole concept. The originality of ACL, he points out, lies not in its parts – 'none of which were actually brought into their first existence by me' – but in their integration into a whole and the application of that whole to training.

'By being brought into a new relation with one another, those parts have undergone varying degrees of transformation, which is inevitable in any creative work.'

Among the constituents borrowed and re-evaluated from earlier gurus are Maslow's 'hierarchy of needs' model and Henri Fayol's classic definitions of management functions. In *Understanding Motivation*, Adair also expounds his 'Fifty-Fifty Rule,' a variation on the Pareto Principle, in which he contends that half an individual's motivation comes from within himself or herself, the other half from external factors, including leadership. This theory contradicts most of the motivation gurus, led by Maslow and Herzberg, who stressed that motivation lies pre-eminently within the individual.

Adair has applied his Fifty-Fifty Rule in other contexts, for example in *Effective Teambuilding* (Gower, 1986), where he suggests that 50 per cent of success depends on the team and 50 per cent on the leader. The Fifty-Fifty Rule has the benefit, he says, of challenging each party to get its performance right before criticizing the quality or contribution of the other. 'It is the ultimate cure to the "Us and Them" disease of organisations.'

KEY BOOKS

Adair, J. (1983) *Effective Leadership*, Aldershot: Gower.
Adair, J. (1986) *Effective Teambuilding*, Aldershot: Gower.
Adair, J. (1988) *Not Bosses But Leaders*, Guildford: Talbot Adair Press.
Adair, J. (1988) *Developing Leaders*, Guildford: Talbot Adair Press.
Adair, J. (1989) *Great Leaders*, Guildford: Talbot Adair Press.
Adair, J. (1990) *Understanding Motivation*, Guildford: Talbot Adair.

(The Talbot Adair imprint is distributed through Kogan Page, London).

H. IGOR ANSOFF

(b.1918)

The theory and practice of strategic planning

Russian–born pioneer of strategic management and corporate planning, whose 1965 book *Corporate Strategy* was described by Henry Mintzberg as 'the most elaborate model of strategic planning in the literature.' Professor Bernard Taylor of Henley Management College, a leading British authority on strategic planning, describes Ansoff as 'the guru's guru' in the field, which he effectively founded in 1963, the year he left Lockheed to teach strategy at Carnegie Institute of Technology. Until that time, Taylor recalls, 'business policy was regarded as a "capstone course" in general management which had no theory to speak of and therefore must be taught entirely by the case method.'

From *Corporate Strategy* (recently republished as *The New Corporate Strategy*), onwards, Ansoff's major books have been milestones in the development of strategic management: *Business Strategy* (1969), *From Strategic Planning to Strategic Management* (1976), *Strategic Management* (1979) and *Implanting Strategic Management* (1984, 1990). The last two, representing a shift from a focus on strategy to the 'bottom line' success of strategic behaviour, have consolidated his leadership in a field that remained underrated, in the UK at least, until the mid-1980s.

Born in Vladivostock of a Russian mother and an

American diplomat father, Ansoff spent his first sixteen years in newly Sovietized Russia. The family then returned to New York, where Ansoff studied mechanical engineering and physics. After service in World War II he took a doctorate in applied mathematics under a government sponsorship scheme for ex-servicemen.

In 1948 Ansoff joined the Rand Foundation, an influential think-tank of the postwar years specializing in military problems. Here he worked on strategic problems of NATO, and the methodology he developed for strategic problem-solving was later to prove a powerful influence on his development of theory and practical technology for business.

Joining the Lockheed aerospace company as a long-range planner gave him a practical outlet when he was appointed to be responsible for Lockheed's diversification. He has said that this job gave him the opportunity to learn how business works and how to identify the key variables and relationships in complex problems. He was promoted to vice-president and general manager in Lockheed Electronics Company where he was faced with the human traumas involved in reducing a division with seventeen high technology businesses down to three, requiring the layoff of 100 engineers. Thus he learned at first hand the difficult part of management, which is managing other people's lives.

Managing a large corporation did not, however, fulfil Ansoff's own long-term career strategy. He became a professor at Carnegie School of Industrial Administration, and shortly after joining Carnegie published his seminal *Corporate Strategy*.

His next move was to become founding dean of the Graduate School of Management at Vanderbilt University in Nashville, Tennessee, where he created a pioneering new business school, based on the concept of strategic management, to train 'change agents.'

Although *Corporate Strategy* received worldwide acceptance, the prescription for strategic planning contained in the book produced mixed results in practice. In some firms it produced significant improvement in performance and became a way of life, but in many others, strategic planning became a phenomenon which Ansoff called 'paralysis by analysis.'

Ansoff decided to find an explanation of this anomaly, a decision which led to 20 years of theoretical and empirical research on successful strategic behaviours. An early step was a four-year research study of success and failure of mergers and acquisitions strategies, the outcome of which was *Acquisition Behaviour of US Manufacturing Firms 1946–1965*, published in 1971. In the following year Ansoff published an article, The Concept of Strategic Management, which argued that explanation of the planning failure must be sought through studying the firm's overall process of strategic management and not just the planning component. Ansoff organized the first international multidisciplinary conference on strategic management, sponsored by IBM and General Electric, at Vanderbilt in 1973. An outcome of this conference was *From Strategic Planning to Strategic Management*, published in 1974.

Ansoff spent the next six years at the Brussels-based European Institute of Advanced Studies in Management, where he led a number of pan-European projects on strategic management and societal strategy and continued his research on strategic management, in particular on the identification of the kinds of strategic behaviour that lead to success in organizations in turbulent environments.

Out of this research came *Strategic Management* (1979), which offered a comprehensive theory of strategic behaviour, and *Implanting Strategic Management* (1984, 1990), which presents a comprehensive practical approach to optimizing strategic behaviour.

Ansoff returned to the US in 1983 to become Distinguished Professor of Strategic Management at US International University, where he created masters' and doctoral level programmes in strategic management. He also formed his own consultancy in San Diego, California.

Igor Ansoff's *Corporate Strategy*, as the author wrote in his preface, seeks 'to develop a practically useful series of concepts and procedures which managers can use to manage . . . a practical method for strategic decision-making within a business firm.'

The book accomplishes this with a methodology of processes and checklists so detailed and rigorous that the former ICI chairman, Sir John Harvey-Jones, introducing the 1986 edition in Sidgwick and Jackson's Library of Management Classics, observed that, using it, 'superficially at least, the corporate strategy could be drawn up by an unintelligent computer . . . .' Harvey-Jones went on to rank the book as 'one of the best business books of all time.'

Professor Bernard Taylor of Henley Management College describes it as 'a brilliant, original contribution, and still an essential introduction to the concept of strategy.' Since the 1970s, however, Ansoff has moved away from the prescriptive approach of the book, which, according to a leading member of Britain's Strategic Planning Society, tended to be interpreted by some of Ansoff's followers in too deterministic a manner ('he preached rigour, not rigidity'). Ansoff's most recent works focus on the necessity of building flexibility and adaptation to change into the planning process.

Corporate Strategy begins by analysing the three main types of decision-making – strategic, administrative and operating – and how they interact. It then explains the specific questions addressed in the strategic category:

- what are the firm's objectives and goals?
- should the firm seek to diversify, in what areas and how vigorously?
- how should the firm develop and exploit its present product-market position?

Ansoff explains that most strategic decisions have to be made within the practical framework of a limited total resource, involving a choice of alternative commitments among resources. Thus, emphasis on current business activity will preclude diversification; over-emphasis on diversification will lead to neglect of present products. 'The object is to produce a resource-allocation pattern which will offer the best potential for meeting the firm's objectives.'

Ansoff next examines how those objectives, both economic and social, can be defined by individual firms according to their own circumstances; moves on to devise a practical method of setting objectives within varying time horizons and of building in enough flexibility to cope with unforeseen calamities or catastrophic change.

'Objectives,' Ansoff writes, 'are a management tool with many potential uses. In the operating problem they can be used for establishing performance standards and objectives for all organisational levels, for appraisal of performance, and for control decisions. In the administrative problem they can be used to diagnose deficiencies in the organisational structure. In our main area of interest, the strategic problem, objectives are used as yardsticks for decisions on changes, deletions and additions to the firm's product-market posture.'

The book then moves into denser thickets of analysis, evolving its own mathematical formulae to demonstrate the meaning of synergy as a component in strategy, applied to acquisitions, start-ups and diversifications. Ansoff follows this by developing a 'concept of strategy' from which a firm can (1) identify the business it should be in, (2) use specific guidelines to search for strategic opportunities and (3) be given decision rules to narrow that selection process down to the most attractive options.

Ansoff preceded Harvard's Michael Porter (qv) by nearly two decades in identifying 'competitive advantage' as a key element in strategic planning. He observed that identifying a competitive advantage requires 'uncommon skills in anticipating trends' to ensure really successful results, and that, because of the need for knowledge of the industries involved, the concentric form of diversification (linked related products and markets) is likely to be more successful than conglomerate diversification.

Corporate Strategy concludes by analysing the pros and

cons of 'make or buy' new product-markets, e.g. whether to plump for organic growth or acquisition.

In summary, *Corporate Strategy* provides both the concepts and practice of strategic decision-making, starting with the philosophical issues that underlie company objectives and progressing to the point at which the firm commits itself to a specific product-market strategy. It finally develops a procedure for appraising and monitoring a strategic project and explains how strategy fits as a management tool into the overall periodic planning process of a firm.

Ansoff's work in Brussels on strategic behaviour patterns and their results on organizations, which was embodied in his theoretical book *Strategic Management*, has been described by him as 'the most important phase of my intellectual development . . . I begged, borrowed and stole concepts and theoretical insights from psychology, sociology and political science. And I attempted to integrate them into a holistic explanation of strategic behaviour.' The centrepiece of the theory presented in that book was the Strategic Success Hypothesis.

While in Brussels he also wrote a series of three important papers (Strategic Issue Management [1980], Managing Strategic Surprise by Response to Weak Signals [1976] and Dispersal Positioning in Strategic Portfolio Analysis [with Kirsch and Roventa, 1980].) These developed a set of practical methods for adapting a firm to fast-changing and unpredictable threats and opportunities.

Implanting Strategic Management, first published in 1984 and updated in 1990, translated the theoretical concepts of the 1979 book into practical 'how to do it' technology. It represents the distillation of Ansoff's 35 years' experience in management (as manager, teacher and consultant) and a culmination of his 20 years' search for a comprehensive explanation of why the original strategic planning failed to work.

Ansoff explains that since the 1960s his thinking developed along three parallel paths: enlargement of his scientific perspective from unidisciplinary to multidisciplinary; the search for a theoretical explanation of strategic behaviour, and development of practical technology for strategic management in turbulent environments.

Implanting Strategic Management is built on the 'strategic success formula' (a practical translation of the strategic success hypothesis), which states that a firm's performance is optimised when its external strategy and internal capability are both matched to the turbulence of the firm's external environment.

The book reports that the strategic success formula has been 'empirically validated' in eight countries around the world, in different industries and in banks.

Implanting Strategic Management represents the most comprehensive exposition of concepts and practical techniques current in strategic management, and recommends processes for creating a dual system within a firm which can both manage strategic change and the daily profit-making activities.

Since his return to the US in 1983, Ansoff has been developing further his work on strategic behaviour, with particular emphasis on patterns that lead to success – most crucially, the ability to manage strategic responses to a turbulent external environment – and on helping firms to behave successfully in strategic terms. He claims that the strategic success formula demonstrates that the days of simple, universal management prescriptions are over, and that each organization must work out its own best solution, whose complexity is neither higher nor lower than the complexity of the firm's environment. Ansoff offers *Implanting Strategic Management* as a tool for finding this solution.

Professor Taylor says Ansoff's work has 'educated and enthused a whole generation of practitioners, consultants and academics in the USA and around the world.' Throughout his distinguished academic career, 'he has kept his contact with practice, working with top management teams in leading multinational companies – always bringing new and original ideas, expressed with energy and enthusiasm.'

KEY BOOKS

Ansoff, H. I. (1965) *Corporate Strategy*, New York: McGraw Hill; (1986) London: Sidgwick and Jackson.

Ansoff, H. I. (1969) *Business Strategy*, London: Penguin Books.

Ansoff, H. I. (1971) *Behavior of US Manufacturing Firms 1946–65* (with R. J. Brandenburg, F. E. Portner, H. R. Radosevich), Nashville: Vanderbilt University Press.

Ansoff, H. I. (1976) *From Strategic Planning to Strategic Management* (with R. Hays, R. Declerck), New York and London: John Wiley and Sons.

Ansoff, H. I. (1979) *Strategic Management*, London: Macmillan.

Ansoff, H. I. (1984, 1990) *Implanting Strategic Management*, New Jersey: Prentice-Hall.

3

CHRIS ARGYRIS

(b.1923)

*Developing individual potential within
the organization*

US organizational psychologist whose special area is the
personal development of individuals within organizations,
and the defence mechanisms that managers often unwittingly use to resist change.

One of the squadron of eminent management thinkers
associated with Harvard University, he has been James
Bryant Conant Professor of Educational and Organiza-
tional Behaviour there since 1971. Before that he was
Professor of Industrial Administration at rival Yale
University.

Argyris has also worked as a consultant in industry,
notably for IBM, Shell and Du Pont, as well as for various
departments of the US government and for governments
in Europe.

Peter Drucker has called organization theorists like Argyris
'romantics' for hoping that by encouraging the principle of
participation they can disprove the anarchist assertion that
'organization is alienation.'

Drucker himself has no such ideals. 'Authority is an
essential dimension of work,' he wrote in *Management:
Tasks, Responsibilities, Practices* (1973). 'It has little or nothing

to do with ownership of the means of production, democracy at the workplace, worker representation or any other way of structuring the "system". It is inherent in the fact of organisation.'

Argyris starts from the premise that each individual has a potential that can be developed – or stultified – by the organization and the particular group circumstances in which he or she works. Developing a person's full potential should be to the benefit of both the individual and the organization, his argument runs, but managers and even peer groups within the organization often lack the 'interpersonal confidence' to allow this to flourish. Managers in particular, he warns, may develop defensive mechanisms to protect their control over others.

In an article for *Harvard Business Review* in which Argyris studied six companies and observed 265 decision-making meetings, he concluded that executive behaviour often creates an atmosphere of distrust and inflexibility, despite the fact that the executives involved genuinely believe trust and innovation to be crucial to good decision-making.

Argyris observed that such discrepancies were not restricted to business organizations: he had obtained similar patterns of behaviour from leaders in education, research, the church, trade unions and government.

His solution was for executives to try asking important 'feedback' questions, at quiet and non-risky times when the pressure was off, discussing tapes of their own meetings and actively entering a learning process about their own behaviour and that of their group.

He identified three basic values that affected his study groups:

- 'The significant human relationships are the ones which have to do with achieving the organisation's objective.' In other words, executives concentrated their efforts on 'getting the job done', often using this as an excuse to avoid probing into workers' interpersonal factors and how groups were getting on together.
- 'Cognitive rationality is to be emphasised; feelings and emotions are to be played down.' Thus interpersonal

relations are viewed as irrelevant, not real work.

- 'Human relationships are most effectively influenced through unilateral direction, coercion and control, as well as by rewards and penalties that sanction all three values.' Direction and control are accepted, Argyris found, as an inevitable, unquestioned part of the managerial chain of command.

The whole suppressed awareness of what senior management was doing was summed up by Argyris: 'During the study of the decision-making processes of the president and the nine vice-presidents of a firm with nearly 3,000 employees, I concluded that the members unknowingly behaved in such a way as not to encourage risk-taking, openness, expression of feelings and cohesive, trusting relationships.'

But in later interviews, the executives claimed that negative feelings were not expressed because 'we trust each other and respect each other.' The reasons why issues of conflict were ignored at meetings included such explanations as: "we should not air our dirty linen in front of people who may come in to make a presentation," and "when people are emotional, they are not rational."

A similar pattern of misinterpreted signals emerged from studies of executives' relationships with middle managers, most of the latter feeling that they did not know where they stood with their bosses and that conflicts were very rarely tackled.

'One key to group and organisational effectiveness is to get this knowledge (that a group was decaying) out into the open and to discuss it thoroughly. The human "motors" of the group and the organisation have to be checked periodically, just as does the motor of an automobile. Without proper maintenance, all will fail.' (*Harvard Business Review*: 'Interpersonal Barriers to Decision-Making.')

Argyris worked with Donald A. Schon on examining how organizations cope with the contradictory goals of maintaining a stable status quo and adapting to change. (*Organizational Learning: A Theory of Action Perspective.*)

How, for example, do members of an organization recon-
cile such opposing messages in their culture as: take
initiatives but keep to the rules; think ahead but remember
that pay is linked to present performance; co-operate with
others but be ready to compete with them?

Argyris and Schon developed what they call Model I to
demonstrate how managers resolve these contradictions.
What they do is to concentrate on setting goals as an
individual; on being as self-contained as possible; on
keeping negative feelings to themselves and on discouraging
others from speaking their minds about matters that worry
them. In this way they hope to protect their own positions
and to deflect issues that could build up a head of steam in
other people.

The primary aim of Model I managers is to defend
themselves and their positions from change while imposing
change where necessary on others. Where they fail,
however, is in creating mistrust and repression. The process
is self-perpetuating because they learn nothing except the
importance of conforming. This is described by Argyris as
'single-loop' learning. The prescription he and Schon
worked out for Model II management proposes 'double-
loop' learning, which takes an opposite course: here the
manager acts on information (once assured that it is valid),
invites free discussion and choice and is prepared to change.
Double-loop learning involves learning from others rather
than from one's own self-perpetuating experience.

To switch managers from Model I to Model II thinking,
Argyris advises a training programme for managers using
interpersonal consultants.

He is fully aware of the difficulties involved in making
the change. In *Strategy, Change and Defensive Routines*, he
writes: 'Top management believes that to change defensive
routines is the equivalent of changing the world, a belief that
I share with them. They conclude that the most realistic
solution is to bypass them . . . .'

Argyris explains that organizations can perform well in
spite of defensive routines operating within them: indeed,
defensive managers are usually loyal, hard-working and
dedicated. The best advice in tackling defensive routines,

says Argyris, is 'to move slowly and iteratively. Let the organisation learn from each experiment so it can make the next one even more successful and build up organisational intelligence on these change processes that can be disseminated throughout the organisation.'

Defensive routines are one strong reason why changing the existing culture in organizations rarely lasts, however. In Argyris' view, 'defensive routines pollute the system and undermine it the same way air pollution undermines our lives.'

KEY BOOKS

Argyris, C. (1957) *Personality and Organization*, New York: Harper and Row.

Argyris, C. (1965) *Organization and Innovation*, Toronto: Irwin.

Argyris, C. and Schon, D. A. (1978) *Organizational Learning: A Theory of Action Perspective*, Wokingham: Addison-Wesley.

Argyris, C. (1985) *Strategy, Change and Defensive Routines*, London: Pitman.

4

CHESTER BARNARD

(1886–1961)

Managing the values of the organization

New England-born Chester Barnard was a rarity among management gurus in being a full-time business executive. He spent 40 years with the Bell Telephone Company and eventually became president of New Jersey Bell.

Barnard was one of the first to study the process of decision-making in organizations, the relationships between formal and informal organizations, and the role and function of the executive. His 1938 book *The Functions of the Executive* exerted tremendous influence in its time: in it, he identified what we now call 'Organization Man,' stating that 'the most important single contribution required of the executive, certainly the most universal qualification, is loyalty, domination by the organisation personality.'

Barnard saw business organizations as more effective instruments of social progress than either church or state, partly because they were driven by the cooperation of individuals working to a common purpose rather than by authority.

Barnard's work also encompassed pioneering thinking on the nature of leadership, upon which others have built, and on corporate culture and value-shaping, a good 30 years before the rest of the management world woke up to their importance. The real role of the chief executive, he suggested, was to manage the values of the organization, as well as to secure employee commitment. **Peters and Waterman in their** *In Search of Excellence* **paid tribute to Barnard's work as 'probably the first balanced treatment of the management process.'**

In the late 1930s, the work of Chester Barnard and Elton Mayo challenged the long-established theories of Max Weber (qv), who defined (and admired) the organization as bureaucracy, and F. W. Taylor (qv), who believed that management could be made an exact science, capable of being applied by a set of rules.

Barnard recognized that organizations are made up of individual human beings with individual motivations, and that every large formal organization carries within it a host of smaller, less formal groupings whose goals need to be harnessed to those of the parent body. This linkage Barnard saw as the responsibility of management. He made an important distinction between management effectiveness and management efficiency, and argued that to be effective, an organization's purpose or goals must be accepted by all the contributors to its system of effort. The willingness of all concerned to co-operate in a common purpose was essential, Barnard considered, to an organization's survival.

For a businessman of his time, Barnard was remarkably percipient in the message he constantly reiterated: that authority in an organization only exists insofar as the people in that organization are willing to accept it. Hence his emphasis on the value of communications, and his three basic principles for ensuring their effectiveness:

- Everyone should know what the channels of communication are.
- Everyone should have access to a formal channel of communication.
- Lines of communication should be as short and direct as possible.

The functions of managers, Barnard believed, were to establish and manage that system of communications; to motivate employees towards the organization's goals, and to formulate those goals in a clearly communicable way. *In Search of Excellence* pinpoints Barnard's contribution to the theory of corporate culture (then barely in its infancy) and the role of the executive within it. 'Barnard was . . . the first (we know of) to talk about the primary role of the chief executive as the shaper and manager of shared values in an organisation,' wrote Peters and Waterman.

Barnard's emphasis on managing the corporate whole was still an unusual concept at the time Peters and Waterman were writing in the early 1980s. He was alone among his contemporaries in sensing 'the unconventional and critical role of executives in making it all happen,' the *Excellence* authors observed. In the preface to *The Functions of the Executive*, Barnard stated that his primary aim was to provide a comprehensive theory of cooperative behaviour in formal organizations.

Barnard's contribution to leadership theory is bound up with this concept of the good manager as value shaper. He contrasted this concept with that of the authoritarian, manipulative manager working strictly on a system of rewards and short-term efficiency. But his theories, as Peters and Waterman pointed out, lay virtually dormant for 30 years while most management thinking concentrated on structure and its relation to postwar growth.

The fact that his vision of an organization is essentially one of desired equilibrium – a state sought by all leading management theorists until comparatively recently – has led to a critical reassessment by those gurus like Richard Pascale (qv) of *Managing on the Edge*, who believe that the vital organization of today must welcome change, discontinuity and even conflict within itself, and manage those things creatively. Pascale points out that Barnard advocates 'coherence among such elements as values, informal social networks, formal systems and purposes. The better they are orchestrated, the better the organisation performs.'

Some of Barnard's disciples, notably Jay Lorsch of Harvard, have filled this gap by evolving 'contingency theory.' But on the whole, Barnard's theories are deemed to be as relevant today as they were in the late 1930s. Despite this, his work is largely neglected, perhaps because some of his books, especially *The Functions of the Executive*, are written in a fairly impenetrable style. Peters and Waterman call it 'virtually unreadable,' but they have no doubt that it remains a monument in management theory.

KEY BOOKS

Barnard, C. (1938) *The Functions of the Executive*, Cambridge, Mass.: Harvard University Press.
Barnard, C. (1948) *Organization and Management*, Cambridge, Mass.: Harvard University Press.

5

WARREN BENNIS

(b.1925)

*'Managers do things right. Leaders do the
right thing'*

New York-born industrial psychologist and adviser to
four US presidents, best known as a guru of leadership
theory, though his earlier work was concerned with
organizational development. He is famous for his aphorism: 'Managers do things right. Leaders do the right
thing.'

Like Abraham Maslow (qv) and Britain's Charles
Handy (qv), Bennis was strongly influenced while at
MIT's Sloan School of Management by Douglas McGregor (qv) and his 'Theory X and Theory Y'. Like Maslow,
he attempted to put Theory Y into action in a practical
management setting – upgrading the run-down University
of Buffalo in the late 1960s – and found that it would not
work without a stiffening framework of structure, direction and controls.

His vision of the organization of the future in *The
Temporary Society* (1968) identified the need for 'adhocracy' (free-moving project teams) – a principle espoused
by Alvin Toffler in *Future Shock*, by Henry Mintzberg
(qv) and most recently by Robert H. Waterman Jr.

From 1971 to 1977 Bennis was president of the University of Cincinnati, but he has worked internationally in
France, Switzerland and India. He is now professor of
management at the University of Southern California.

For the second of his three works on leadership

(*Leaders: The Strategies for Taking Charge*), which he wrote in 1986 with Burt Nanus, he studied 90 individuals in different parts of US society, including astronaut Neil Armstrong, sports coaches and orchestra conductors as well as businessmen, and identified four factors or 'competencies' common to all – the ability to manage attention, meaning, trust and self.

He believes leadership can be taught and learned and in his latest book, *On Becoming a Leader*, sets out to show how it is done. The best leaders, he says, are 'ideas people, conceptualists.'

Bennis regards himself as more of a journalist than a guru and has an eye for the memorable quote. He is fond of quoting a little-known aphorism by Winston Churchill: 'The emperor of the future will be the emperor of ideas.'

Warren Bennis sees the leader, the person who transforms an organization, as 'the social architect' – a concept anticipated before World War II by Chester Barnard. Tom Peters has acknowledged that, 25 years before *In Search of Excellence*, Bennis had perceived much of what Peters and Waterman identified as landmarks of the excellent company.

In *The Unconscious Conspiracy – Why Leaders Can't Lead*, Bennis pointed up the ability of leaders to bring about change by positive motivation: 'In a study of school teachers, it turned out that when they held high expectations of their students, that alone was enough to cause an increase of 25 points in the students' IQ scores.'

Leadership, says Bennis, is 'probably the most studied and least understood of any management subject.' His favourite definition of the attribute is: 'The capacity to create a compelling vision and translate it into action and sustain it.'

The four key abilities identified in Bennis's 1985 study of 90 successful US public figures are: the management of attention, the management of meaning (communications), the management of trust and the management of self. The first he attributes to a vision that others can believe in and adopt as their own. Vision is about the long term; market imperatives are short term. 'With a vision,' says Bennis, 'the leader provides the all-important bridge from the present to the future of the organisation.' Among examples he cites are Lee Iacocca at Chrysler, President John F. Kennedy and civil rights leader Martin Luther King. (Two of those three, of course, were assassinated; the great and permanent risk of strong political leadership.)

Communicating vision and translating it into successful results for the organization is the second of Bennis' required leadership skills; the management of meaning. This, he explains, is why Ronald Reagan was deemed a more successful president than the better-informed, more thoughtful Jimmy Carter.

The mission credo of Johnson & Johnson translates vision into practical daily guidelines. General Motors under chief executive Roger Smith placed a high value on getting the company's long-term vision shared by all employees.

Trust, the third key factor to leadership skills, is described by Bennis as 'the emotional glue that binds followers and leaders together.' He believes leaders have to be consistent, and in the late 1980s cited Margaret Thatcher as a prime example – 'focused, constant, and all of a piece.'

Self-management, the fourth quality, means persistence, self-knowledge, willingness to take risks, commitment and challenge. Above all, it means willingness to go on learning, and in particular to learn from adversity and failure. 'The learning person looks forward to failures or mistakes. The worst problem in leadership is basically early success.'

In *Leaders*, Bennis and Nanus concluded that the most impressive and memorable quality of the individuals they studied was 'the way they responded to failure . . . They simply don't think about failure, don't even use the word, relying on such synonyms as "mistake", "glitch", "bungle", or countless others.'

Bennis is the acknowledged world guru on leadership theory; although most management writers now include it in their work, only Bennis, John Adair in Britain, Rensis Likert and a handful of lesser American gurus like John

Kotter have specialized in the field.

On Becoming a Leader, Bennis' third and latest work on the subject, addresses itself to three practical questions: how people learn to lead, how an organization can encourage or unwittingly stifle leadership qualities, and how it can be taught. His case studies in this instance are less known than those in the 1985 book, consisting of 29 American personalities from feminists to film-makers. Some critics, including John Adair reviewing the book in *Director* magazine, felt that Bennis missed his mark. The basic message that becoming a leader is synonymous with becoming yourself 'is not a message I can buy,' wrote Adair. 'A measure of self-fulfilment may be a by-product of becoming a leader, but it should neither be the aim nor is it the means of doing so.'

Leaders: the Strategies for Taking Charge, which sold over 300,000 copies and turned Bennis overnight into a world authority on leadership, remains the one to read.

KEY BOOKS

Bennis, W. (1968) *The Temporary Society*, New York: Harper and Row.

Bennis, W. (1976) *The Unconscious Conspiracy*, New York: Amacon Press

Bennis, W. and Nanus, B. (1985) *Leaders: the Strategies for Taking Charge*, New York: Harper and Row.

Bennis, W. (1989) *On Becoming a Leader*, London: Business Books.

6

EDWARD DE BONO

(b.1933)

Lateral thinking: 'the generation of new ideas and the escape from old ones'

Malta-born, Oxford-educated psychology and medical graduate who invented the concept of lateral thinking, now entered in the Oxford English Dictionary as 'seeking to solve problems by unorthodox or apparently illogical methods.'

De Bono is the foremost example of a guru who has built a reputation out of one 'Big Idea'. Describing himself as 'a thinker about thinking,' he has generated 37 books out of his brainwave, along with a highly lucrative career in teaching, lecturing and consultancy.

His central argument, derived from his medical experience, is that humans are quite good at processing with mathematics, statistics and computers, but have done very little about perception and creativity (functions that computers are unable to carry out). It was also from medicine that he derived his ideas of the patterning behaviour of self-organizing systems. His book *The Mechanism of Mind*, published in 1969, was about 20 years ahead of its time.

Among the world-class companies to whom he has acted as consultant are Shell, IBM, Exxon, 3M, Apple, ICI, Citibank, General Foods, Procter & Gamble and Unilever. His International Creative Forum brings together leading corporations in different fields to focus on the introduction of 'serious creativity' into their organizations. He has also been retained by governments and non-business organizations such as police forces and he runs the world's largest curriculum programme for the direct teaching of thinking in schools.

De Bono has taught at Oxford, Cambridge, London and Harvard universities and is the founder-director (since 1971) of the Cognitive Research Trust in Cambridge and the Centre for the Study of Thinking. He now spends much of his time working for the Supranational Independent Thinking Organisation in The Hague.

His books have been translated into 25 languages and his work is academically respected in countries as different as Venezuela and the Soviet Union.

'The purpose of lateral thinking,' says Edward de Bono in *Lateral Thinking for Management* (1971) 'is the generation of new ideas and the escape from old ones.' He likens the process to developing a cross-reference technique for a filing system set up to store data in a particular way. Creativity, he says, 'involves breaking out of established patterns in order to look at things in a different way,' and creativity, he points out, comes into every aspect of managing a business – not only innovation but information systems, communications, finance, marketing, advertising and promotion, labour relations, problem solving, planning, design, R&D and public relations.

De Bono differentiates lateral thinking from 'vertical' or traditional, logical thinking, which proceeds step by step 'directly from one state of information to another state . . . One of the characteristic features of vertical thinking is continuity. One of the characteristic features of lateral thinking is discontinuity.'

The two systems do not cancel each other out, but are complementary. Where vertical thinking operates on a 'Yes/No' progression of alternatives, seeking always the solution that is right, lateral thinking proceeds by provocative leaps in unlikely directions, seeking what can be used in an idea rather than accepting or rejecting the whole idea outright. Quite often both systems come up with the same solution, says de Bono, but one can increase the chances of success by developing skills in lateral thinking.

In practice, he suggests, one could use lateral thinking for five per cent of the time and vertical thinking for the other 95 per cent, operating the systems alternately: 'lateral thinking turns up an idea, vertical thinking develops it.' Vertical thinking comes into its own in testing the creative ideas turned up by lateral thinking, and for transforming them into a plan of action. Lateral thinking, says its inventor, is not a method for decision-making.

De Bono's books on lateral thinking offer a system for teaching oneself the skill. High among his training 'tools' is the 'operational', nonsense-word PO, which acts like a railway signal to switch thinking patterns onto new tracks. In one of de Bono's examples, considering the problem of how to reduce traffic congestion in cities, use of PO triggers the 'intermediate impossible' solution of square wheels for cars. The underlying truth of that is how to make driving difficult or unpleasant and thereby discourage use of cars: more practical solutions could be a tax on road use or physical ridges in the road.

Other 'discontinuity' techniques include the use of analogy and 'random word' association to break the chain of vertical thinking. *Lateral Thinking for Management* also provides guidelines for formal brainstorming sessions and group practices for executives. De Bono summarizes the lateral thinking process in five steps:

- Escape from clichés and fixed patterns;
- Challenge assumptions;
- Generate alternatives;
- Jump to new ideas and then see what happens;
- Find new entry points from which to move forward.

In applying its uses to management, de Bono also looks to a future when the 'concept manager' will have an established role in a corporation, managing the 'concept capital' of the organization – creativity, new ideas, adapting to change, defining objectives. Until that time arrives, he suggests, the organization of lateral thinking as a management tool may fall to the training officer, the OR department, the planning department or R&D. It should not, he stresses, be the special preserve of any one department.

De Bono himself considers his most significant book to be *I Am Right, You Are Wrong* (Viking/Penguin 1990), which he claims challenges the whole basis of the West's thinking culture. It explains the difference between 'rock' and 'water' logic, why rock logic has restricted the full potential of thinking, and how water logic arises from a fuller understanding of how the brain works.

The oddly titled *Six Thinking Hats* (1985) provides a system for escaping from traditional argument and confrontational thinking to better exploration of a subject and a more creative outcome. It has been adopted by major corporations such as IBM, Prudential and Du Pont. De Bono is extending this system (in which imaginary 'hats' in different colours are donned to encourage specific mental functions: e.g. white for information, red for feeling and intuition, black for caution, yellow for benefits, green for creative thinking, blue for the organization of thinking) with a sequel called *Six Action Shoes*, which separates routine from emergency action.

De Bono believes that the usual approach to fostering creativity – relying on inspiration and release from inhibitions – is far too weak, and that the brain, not being naturally creative, requires the exercise of deliberate techniques to stimulate it. Although inevitably overlapping to some extent, his books and courses on thinking represent a genre he has made his own. A basic de Bono library is listed here.

KEY BOOKS

De Bono, E. (1967) *The Use of Lateral Thinking*, Maidenhead: McGraw-Hill; London: Penguin.

De Bono, E. (1968) *The Five-Day Course in Thinking*, Maidenhead: McGraw-Hill; London: Penguin.

De Bono, E. (1969) *The Mechanism of Mind*, Maidenhead: McGraw-Hill; London: Penguin.

De Bono, E. (1971) *Lateral Thinking for Management*, Maidenhead: McGraw-Hill; London: Penguin.

De Bono, E. (1982) *De Bono's Course in Thinking*, Maidenhead: McGraw-Hill; London: Penguin.

De Bono, E. (1985) *Conflicts: A Better Way to Resolve Them*, Maidenhead: McGraw-Hill; London: Penguin.

De Bono, E. (1985) *Tactics: The Art and Science of Success*, Maidenhead: McGraw-Hill; London: Penguin.

De Bono, E. (1985) *Six Thinking Hats*, London: Penguin.

De Bono, E. (1990) *I Am Right, You Are Wrong*, London: Viking

7

ALFRED D. CHANDLER

(b.1918)

Structure follows strategy in organizations

US economic historian, Straus Professor of Business History at Harvard University since 1971, whose work on organizations has been largely based on studies of major US companies between 1850 and 1920; the period, as he sees it, when modern capitalism was shaped and a new economic unit came into being. This was the business with a range of distinct operating units, each managed autonomously and completely different from its historical predecessor, the traditional single-unit firm, personally owned and managed.

Chandler believes that his work contributed to a nationwide restructuring of corporations, with the multi-divisional form of organization becoming the standard for large industrial firms producing multiple products in multiple markets. He was one of the first management theorists to perceive the importance of creating a strategic plan for a business before framing its organizational structure.

His most influential book, *Strategy and Structure*, was used by AT&T executives in their restructuring exercise after the 1984 breakup of the telecommunications giant, and Chandler's theories were credited with helping to speed up the change of focus within AT&T from a service utility to an actively marketed sales organization.

Chandler's main contribution to management theory has been to explain the relationship in organizations between strategy and structure, from which he took the title of his best-known book, published in 1962. In *Strategy and Structure*, he demonstrates how the two are indissolubly linked in an organization, defining 'strategy' as the determination of long-term goals and objectives, courses of action and allocation of resources, and 'structure' as the way the organization is put together to administer the strategy, with all the hierarchies and lines of authority which that implies. Chandler is clear in his belief that structure follows strategy.

Like Weber, he believes that the managerial hierarchy system offers the best hope for long-term business prosperity, and he concentrates on the principle that the salaried manager's role is critical. 'The visible hand' of management, he observes in *Managerial Hierarchies*, replaced Adam Smith's "invisible hand" of market forces by coordinating the flow of goods from producers to customers more efficiently and profitably than was achieved by simple market mechanisms. As managers receive power and authority through their official roles, so their careers become increasingly technical and professional.

Chandler was the first management writer to recognize the importance of the decentralization principle in a large corporation, which became the central tenet of so much business practice in the 1960s and 1970s. It had already contributed substantially to Alfred P. Sloan's restructuring of General Motors in the interwar years, but Sloan did not publish his own book until 1963.

Chandler was also an early advocate of the need to coordinate strategic planning from the centre to ensure long-term growth for the company, while allowing the individual units and their managers to get on with day-to-day tactics.

His guiding rule has always been that outside pressures dictate how firms evolve from Weber-style traditional, family-based businesses into large, hierarchical organizations – pressures born of the huge market expansions and technological changes of the late nineteenth and early twentieth centuries. He traces the first managerial hierarchies to the rapid expansion of US railroads in the 1850s and 1860s, when a need emerged for centralized scheduling but local management of a variety of functions in geographic divisions that were responsible for up to 100 miles of track.

In his studies of four great US corporations – General Motors, Sears Roebuck, Du Pont and Standard Oil – Chandler looks at how these companies responded to similar external pressures either by positive strategies such as seeking new markets or diversifying products, or by negative, defensive strategies such as vertical integration with suppliers to protect a market position.

Some were more successful than others: Standard Oil, in Chandler's view, was slow to respond with a decentralized structure in the 1920s because of a failure to understand how structure should follow strategy.

Chandler's analysis of corporate development in the different markets and economies of Europe as well as in the US have led him to conclude that 'only by comparing the evolution of large-scale multi-unit enterprises in different economies can organizational imperatives be identified and the impact of the cultural attitudes and values, ideologies, political systems, and social structures that affect these imperatives be understood.'*

In each case, however, the structure of a management hierarchy followed the creation of the multi-unit business and enabled it to function through delegation of responsibility.

*From *Managerial Hierarchies*: Comparative Perspectives on the Rise of Modern Industrial Enterprises, ed. by A. D. Chandler and H. Deams (Harvard University Press, 1980), quoted in *Organizational Theory*, ed. D. S. Pugh (Penguin, 1990)

KEY BOOKS

Chandler, A. D. (1962) *Strategy and Structure*, Massachusetts: MIT Press.

Chandler, A. D. (1977) *The Visible Hand: The Managerial Revolution in American Business*, Cambridge, Mass.: Harvard University Press.

Chandler, A. D. and Deams, H. (eds) (1980) *Managerial Hierarchies: Comparative Perspectives on the Rise of Modern Industrial Enterprises*, Cambridge, Mass.: Harvard University Press.

Chandler, A. D. and Tedlow, R. S. (1985) *The Coming of Managerial Capitalism*, Toronto: Irwin.

8

W. EDWARDS DEMING

(b.1900)

The key to quality: reducing variation

US statistician and founding father of the quality movement, who was responsible, with his fellow-American
Joseph Juran, for instilling the quality philosophy into
postwar Japanese industry. The message had been
rejected or ignored by American companies and was only
re-imported after Japanese manufacturing began its competitive march into American markets.

Deming and Juran remain icons of Japanese industry,
whose companies compete annually for a Deming Prize,
awarded since 1951 for major improvements in quality.
Both men were honoured by the Emperor with the Order
of the Sacred Treasure, second class, the highest Japanese
award ever given to foreigners.

Deming is regarded by the Japanese as the chief architect
of their phenomenal industrial success, but his home
country only began to recognize him in 1980, as a result of
an NBC television documentary on Japanese industry
called 'If Japan Can, Why Can't We?' Overnight, American
industry discovered his existence. Now he is revered
internationally for his simple yet revolutionary principle
that all processes are vulnerable to loss of quality through
variation: if the levels of variation are managed, they can
be decreased and quality raised. Deming still holds about
20 four-day seminars every year and teaches once a week
at Columbia University, New York.

After US industry finally woke up to Deming's theories, several large corporations suffering intractable problems came to credit Deming as the key to their revival; most notably Ford Motor Company in the early 1970s. Nashua Corporation in New Hampshire, a Fortune 500 company making computer disks, copiers and other office products, was one of the first Western companies to adopt Deming's principles. Nashua subsequently managed to cut its order-entry lead times from eight days to one hour and achieved a 70 per cent reduction in customer claims.

William E. Conway, Nashua's president and later chief executive officer, who 'discovered' Deming when the guru was 78, has called him 'the father of the Third Wave of the Industrial Revolution' for the way in which he developed statistical control of quality levels into a new way of managing business. 'The Japanese manufacturers utilising the statistical control of quality are sweeping the world in the second half of the 20th century, just as American manufacturers utilising mass production swept the world in the first half,' said Conway.

In the UK, Sir John Egan applied Deming principles to turning round the ailing fortunes of Jaguar Cars in the early 1980s. Egan wrote of Deming's 1986 book *Out of the Crisis* that it was 'required reading for every chief executive in British industry who is serious about ensuring the international competitiveness of his company.' (*Director* Magazine, September 1988).

Deming, an electrical engineer by training (University of Wyoming, 1921) and a Ph.D. in mathematical physics from Yale, worked for a time in the 1920s at the Western Electric Hawthorne plant in Chicago where Elton Mayo carried out his famous experiments in communication and motivation. Here Deming discovered the work of Walter Shewhart, the pioneer of controlled and uncontrolled variables and the statistical control of processes. He later became a statistician for the US government, working on data for the national census of 1939/40. In 1942 he set up courses to teach Shewhart's methods to industrialists and engineers. After the war he was invited to Japan by General MacArthur to advise on the Japanese census. Contacts made then resulted in the watershed invitation of 1950 which was to have such reverberating effects.

Deming's approach to quality control is basically that of a statistician (his compatriot and fellow quality guru J. M. Juran has criticized him for it), but it is also firmly rooted in the belief that quality is about people, not products – an approach which made a particular impact on the Japanese. He also believes that 85 per cent of production faults are the responsibility of management, not workers. The famous Deming 'Fourteen Points' of management are at the heart of his philosophy.

In 1950, when W. Edwards Deming made his first visit to Japan, the country was still recovering from the atomic bombing raids of August 1945. The economy was struggling to stand upright, much less move ahead, and Japanese goods still suffered from their prewar reputation for shoddiness.

Deming embarked on an exhausting series of lectures to engineers, from 8am to 5pm day after day in punishing heat. 'I was dripping wet by 8.30am,' he recalled in the BBC2 television series *Nippon*. 'The Japanese appreciated it. They were sorely afraid that they had established a reputation for shoddy quality and that they could never undo it. I assured them that it would take only a short while to undo that reputation and develop a new one.

'I think I was the only man in Japan in 1950 who believed my prediction – that within five years manufacturers the world over would be screaming for protection. It took four years.'

The core element in this apparent miracle was the 'management circle' – still known in Japan as the 'Deming circle' – of planning, implementation, check and action. Above all, it rested on the belief in 'Management for Quality' (Deming uses this term where Juran 'brands' his approach as 'Company-Wide Quality'.)

Deming's basic management philosophy, as impressed on his eager Japanese audiences, was to regard the consumer as 'the most important part of the production line.' Developing this in *Out of the Crisis* (1984), he insisted that merely having a satisfied customer was not enough. 'Profit in business comes from repeat customers, customers that boast about your product and service, and that bring friends with them.'

Deming also teaches the necessity of staying ahead of the customer, anticipating what his needs will be in years to come.

His Fourteen Points for management were developed over some twenty years and are still being refined and re-worded by the master. Henry Neave, author of *The Deming Dimension* (SPC Press, Knoxville, 1990), explains that they are not instructions or techniques, but rather 'vehicles for opening up the mind to new thinking, to the possibility that there are radically different and better ways of organizing our businesses and working with people.'

These, as quoted in Neave's book and Deming's own words, are the basic Fourteen Points:

1. Create constancy of purpose for continual improvement of products and service.
2. Adopt the new philosophy created in Japan.
3. Cease dependence on mass inspection: build quality into the product in the first place.
4. End lowest-tender contracts; instead, require meaningful measures of quality along with price.
5. Improve constantly and forever every process for planning, production and service.
6. Institute modern methods of training on the job for all, including management.
7. Adopt and institute leadership aimed at helping people to do a better job.
8. Drive out fear, encourage effective two-way communication.
9. Break down barriers between departments and staff areas.
10. Eliminate exhortations for the workforce – they only create adversarial relationships.
11. Eliminate quotas and numerical targets. Substitute aid

and helpful leadership.
12. Remove barriers to pride of workmanship, including annual appraisals and Management by Objectives.
13. Encourage education and self-improvement for everyone.
14. Define top management's permanent commitment to ever-improving quality and productivity, and their obligation to implement all these principles.

The Fourteen Points are comprehensively expounded, chapter by chapter, in *The Deming Dimension*, a fascinating exposition of the guru's work and its development since publication of *Out of the Crisis*.

Deming himself has said: 'If I had to reduce my message for management to just a few words, I'd say it all had to do with reducing variation.'

KEY BOOKS

Deming, W. E. (1982) *Quality, Productivity and Competitive Position*, Massachusetts: MIT, Center for Advanced Engineering Study.
Deming, W. E. (1986, 1988) *Out of the Crisis*, Massachusetts: MIT, Center for Advanced Engineering Study; Cambridge: Cambridge University Press.
Walton, Mary. (1986, 1989) *The Deming Management Method* New York: Dodd, Mead and Co.; London: Mercury Books.
Neave, H. R. (1990) *The Deming Dimension*, Knoxville, Tennessee: SPC Press; available in the UK through the British Deming Association, 2 Castle Street, Salisbury, Wilts SP1 1BB

9

PETER DRUCKER

(b.1909)

Primary tasks for effective managers

The management guru's management guru. Born in Vienna during the heyday of that city's pre-1914 culture, Drucker has invented or prefigured most of the leading management theories of the last half-century, from 'Management By Objectives' to privatization; from putting the customer first to the role of the chief executive in corporate strategy; from 'structure follows strategy' to 'stick to the knitting'; from decentralization to the implications of the information age.

His five basic principles of management remain as valid as ever: setting objectives, organizing, motivating and communicating, establishing measurements of performance and developing people.

Tom Peters, whose co-authored book *In Search of Excellence* developed many Drucker ideas, says the Viennese sage deserves much of the credit for 'moving 75 to 80 per cent of the Fortune 500 to radical decentralisation,' adding that no true 'discipline of management' existed before Drucker.

For many years a pillar of New York University Business School, Drucker since 1971 has been Clarke Professor of Social Science at Claremont Graduate School, Claremont, California. He is still writing prolifically in his eighties, adding to the 24-odd books he has published since *The End of Economic Man* appeared in

1939. They divide almost equally between works on management theory and technique and works of economic, political and social analysis. Many of the latter are seminal works which mapped out whole landscapes of the future with much wider horizons than those bounded by management. Philip Sadler, vice-president and former director of Ashridge Management College, found his thinking entirely changed by Drucker's 1969 book *The Age of Discontinuity*, which for Sadler pointed clearly to the coming decline of Britain's manufacturing industry.

This book, still well worth study, prefigured many of the business best-sellers of the late 1980s and early 1990s on managing chaos and disruptive change. Drucker's books have anticipated those of Charles Handy (qv), Tom Peters (qv) and Richard Pascale (qv) – to name only three. In some of its ideas, *The Age of Discontinuity* was 20 years ahead of John Naisbitt's *Megatrends* and Charles Handy's *The Age of Unreason*.

It was in *The Age of Discontinuity*, incidentally, that Drucker introduced the concept of privatization, though he called it 'reprivatization.' He accurately forecast the disillusionment with government arising from the discovery that governments could not, after all, produce miracles. 'There is little doubt, for instance, that the British in adopting the National Health Service believed that medical care would cost nothing . . . . Nurses, doctors, hospitals, drugs and so on have to be paid for by somebody. But everybody expected this "somebody" to be somebody else.'

Drucker advocated privatization on the grounds that the purpose of government was to govern, not to 'do', and that the two roles were incompatible. His vision, unlike the Conservative Party's realization of it, was for privatization to cover all institutions, not merely business ones – universities, for example.

A year or so after publication of *The Age of Discontinuity*, the word privatization made its first appearance in a Conservative Central Office pamphlet, in May 1970 ('A New Style of Government'), crediting Drucker with the coinage.

The son of an Austrian government official who helped found the Salzburg Festival, Drucker came to Britain in the late 1920s, and his first job was as an apprentice clerk in a Bradford wool exporting firm, working with a quill pen in 80-pound brassbound ledgers chained to the desk. Between 1933 and 1936 he worked as an economist in a London merchant bank and then decided to throw in his lot with the United States. He emigrated to the US in 1937, produced his first book two years later and in 1942 took a consultant's job with General Motors, then the world's largest company.

Out of this experience came his influential 1946 book *Concept of the Corporation*, still one of the best and most perceptive analyses of the successful large organization. As well as General Motors, other companies studied in the book were General Electric, IBM and Sears Roebuck, and Drucker identified their success with certain managerial characteristics, notably delegation and goal-setting (Management by Objectives) and certain structural characteristics, such as decentralization.

Drucker believed that the ultimate key to success in all these companies was that 'they knew what businesses they were in, what their competencies were and how to keep their efforts focused on their goals.' (*Organization Theory*, ed. D. S. Pugh) Nearly 30 years later Peters and Waterman reached much the same conclusion, set out in more populist style, in their best-seller *In Search of Excellence*.

Concept of the Corporation also analysed the importance of marketing – at that time an almost universally neglected function – and the delicate balance which a company must seek to achieve between long-term strategy and short-term performance.

Drucker figures in more management-book indexes than any other individual by far. In *Makers of Management*, by David Clutterbuck and Stuart Crainer, he rates no fewer than 40 separate page references.

Peter Drucker's reputation as a management guru was established with *The Practice of Management* (1954), a work still regarded by later theorists as one of the best and clearest in the field. In this, he identified management by objectives as the first of seven primary tasks of management. MBO, dignified with capital letters, became a movement of its own, and Britain's John Humble (qv) made a speciality of developing its theory and practice.

Management by objectives emerged out of Drucker's work with General Electric among his studies for *Concept of the Corporation*. Each GE manager was responsible for a profit centre and given targets to achieve – seven per cent return on sales and 20 per cent return on investment. These were severely applied; you lost your job if you didn't meet them.

Drucker perceived that, since businesses survive or fall by the bottom line, corporate goals should be divided into objectives and clearly assigned to units and individuals. 'Management by objectives,' as Richard Pascale observes in *Managing on the Edge*, 'ensures that each link in the chain of command does its part . . .'

A subsequent handbook, *Managing for Results* (1964) is, in Drucker's own words of introduction, a 'what to do book.' It was, he believed, 'the first attempt at an organized presentation of the economic tasks of the business executive and the first halting step towards a discipline of economic performance in business enterprise.' It sets out in clear, no-nonsense prose, guidelines for understanding business realities and for analysing a company in terms of revenues, resources, prospects, cost centres, customer needs, building on strengths, finding potential, making key decisions and building strategies for the future. It is still one of the best practical vade-mecums for anyone running a business enterprise. Drucker believes that every three years or so a company should be put under the microscope and every product, process, technology, service or market subjected to a gruelling assessment.

Throughout his work, Drucker's emphasis has been on the effectiveness of managers – particularly in making good use of their human resources – as the key to a productive and profitable organization. Management, says Drucker, is the job of organizing resources to achieve the satisfactory performance of an enterprise. Managers must in the end be measured by their economic performance, though this is not necessarily synonymous with maximum profits; rather, with sufficient profit that will cover the risks which have been taken, and to avoid the enterprise making a loss. Management by objectives is the key to this.

Drucker has sometimes been criticized for neglecting theories of motivation, though he was one of the first to recognize and praise Douglas McGregor's Theory Y of consultative management as early as 1954.

Drucker's emphasis on objective-setting for management is most clearly set out in his mammoth compendium *Management: Tasks, Responsibilities, Practices* (1973). This represents an encyclopedia of his earlier writings and is recommended as the bedrock of any aspiring manager's reading list. Studded with illuminating case studies, the massive volume (weighing 3½ pounds in hardback) defines every aspect of managerial skills and pinpoints eight areas where clear objectives are vital: marketing, innovation, human organization, financial resources, physical resources, productivity, social responsibility and profit requirements. A thorough grounding in this vast work is virtually the equivalent of a do-it-yourself business-school course.

Shortly before this was published, Drucker had defined his broad view of management in *People and Performance* (1973): 'To fulfil the specific purpose and mission of the organization; to make work productive and the worker achieving; and to manage social impacts and social responsibility.'

In *Management: Tasks, Responsibilities, Practices*, he identified five basic operations in the work of the manager, which together 'result in the integration of resources into a viable growing organism.' These summarize the essentials of management with more clarity than any other book before or since:

'A manager, in the first place, sets objectives. He determines what the objectives should be. He determines what the goals in each area of objectives should be. He decides what has to be done to reach these objectives. He makes the objectives effective by communicating them to the people whose performance is needed to attain them.

'Second, a manager organises. He analyses the activities, decisions and relations needed. He classifies the work. He divides it into manageable activities and further divides the activities into manageable jobs. He groups these units and jobs into an organisation structure. He selects people for the management of these units and for the jobs to be done.

'Next, a manager motivates and communicates. He makes a team out of the people that are responsible for various jobs. He does that through the practices with which he works. He does it in his own relations to the men with whom he works. He does it through his "people decisions" on pay, placement and promotion. And he does it through constant communication, to and from his subordinates, and to and from his superior, and to and from his colleagues.

'The fourth basic element in the work of the manager is measurement. The manager establishes yardsticks – and few factors are as important to the performance of the organisation and of every man in it. He sees to it that each man has measurements available to him which are focused on the performance of the whole organisation and which, at the same time, focus on the work of the individual and help him do it. He analyses, appraises and interprets performance. As in all other areas of his work, he communicates the meaning of the measurements and their findings to his subordinates, to his superiors, and to colleagues.

'Finally, a manager develops people, including himself.

Taking an historical perspective, Drucker has since identified seven key elements in postwar management development:

1. Scientific management of work as the key to productivity;

2. Decentralization as a basic principle of organization;
3. Personnel management as the orderly way of fitting people into organization structures;
4. Manager development to provide for the needs of tomorrow;
5. Managerial accounting – use of analysis and information as the foundation for firm decision-making;
6. Marketing;
7. Long-range planning.

In recent years, Drucker's books have included *Innovation and Entrepreneurship* (1985), a typically wide-ranging study of growth sectors of the US economy in the early 1980s, including many businesses not normally considered as such: private health care, for example, non–profit-making private schools and public/private partnerships in which government units contract out services to competitive private companies. *The New Realities* (1989) ranged over a global stage, anticipating the development of such contemporary phenomena as the transnational economy, the democratization of the Soviet republics, the changing ethos of the United States and the demands of a post-industrial, post-business society.

Drucker's breadth of vision and eclectic range of publications spring from his belief that management is central to life, not merely to business. One of his recurring concepts is that of the chief executive as conductor of an orchestra. As he says: 'We are beginning to realise that management itself is the central institution of our present society, and that there are very few differences between managing a business, managing a diocese, managing a hospital, managing a university, managing a research lab, managing a labour union or managing a government agency. All along, this has been the main thrust of my work, and the one that distinguishes it from practically all my contemporaries working in the field.'

Rosabeth Moss Kanter (qv) views his goals as even more embracing. In an article in *New Management* (winter 1985), she wrote: 'Good management is also our best hope for world peace. In the Drucker perspective, imperatives for

47

growth push organisations beyond national borders in the search for new markets. The world becomes inter-connected by a series of cross-cutting trade relationships in which the interests of managers in the survival of their multinational enterprises outweigh the interests of politicians. Quality of life, technological progress and world peace, then, are all the products of good management . . . At root, Drucker is a management utopian, descended as much from Robert Owen as Max Weber.'

To Drucker, the business organization, as any organization, is 'a human, a social, indeed a moral phenomenon.' Customer service rather than profit should dominate management thinking, profit being the means of continued investment in innovation and improvement.

'Contrary to the approach to the study of political and social organisation that has prevailed in the West since Machiavelli, I stressed all along that organisation does not deal with power but with responsibility. This is the keynote of my work that has remained constant over more than 40 years.'

Drucker sums up his own vast contribution to management thinking in these words, quoted in *Makers of Management* (Clutterbuck and Crainer):

'I was the first one to see that the purpose of a business lies outside of itself – that is, in creating and satisfying a customer. I was the first to see the decision process as central, the first to see that structure has to follow strategy, and the first one to see, or at least the first to say, that management has to be management by objectives and self-control.'

KEY BOOKS

Drucker, P. F. (1946) *Concept of the Corporation*, New York: John Day.
Drucker, P. F. (1951) *The New Society*, London: Heinemann.
Drucker, P. F. (1954) *The Practice of Management*, New

York: Harper and Row.

Drucker, P. F. (1964, 1989) *Managing for Results*, London: Heinemann.

Drucker, P. F. (1969) *The Age of Discontinuity*, London: Heinemann.

Drucker, P. F. (1974) *Management: Tasks, Responsibilities, Practices*, London: Heinemann; New York: Harper and Row.

Drucker, P. F. (1985) *Innovation and Entrepreneurship*, London: Heinemann.

Drucker, P. F. (1989, 1990) *The New Realities*, London: Heinemann Professional Publishing; Mandarin Paperback.

10

HENRI FAYOL

(1841–1925)

Five foundation stones of modern management

French mining engineer and manager, generally regarded as the first to ask 'what is management?', to analyse the nature of managerial activity and to formulate a complete theory of management, based on his own experience of running the mining and metallurgical combine Commentry-Fourchamboult-Decazeville.

Fayol was in his seventies before his ideas gained currency in print, and his classic work, *Administration Industrielle et Générale*, was not published in English (as *General and Industrial Management*) until 1949. His key definitions of managerial activity – to plan, to organize, to command, to coordinate and to control – remained accepted wisdom until Henry Mintzberg's revealing studies in the 1960s.

Henry Fayol was years ahead of his time in linking strategy and organizational theory and in emphasizing the need for management development and the qualities of leadership. Igor Ansoff in *Corporate Strategy* (1965) said that Fayol 'anticipated imaginatively and soundly most of the more recent analyses of modern business practice,' although Peter Drucker in his great compendium *Management: Tasks,*

Responsibilities and Practice (1973), criticized the application of Fayol's functional approach to larger and more complex organizations than the one he knew and managed.

Fayol believed the same principles of management could be applied, regardless of size, to organizations of all kinds, whether industrial, commercial, governmental, political, or even religious. His five key elements of industrial management remain the foundation-stones on which all later gurus, to a greater or lesser extent, have built.

These five elements are: to forecast and plan; to organize; to command; to coordinate and to control. Fayol defined the first as 'examining the future and drawing up the plan of action'; the second as 'building up the structure, material and human, of the undertaking'; the third as 'maintaining activity among the personnel'; the fourth as 'binding together, unifying and harmonising all activity and effort,' and the fifth as 'seeing that everything occurs in conformity with established rule and expressed command.'

An organization, therefore, begins with a strategic plan or definition of goals, progresses to a structure to put that plan into action, is carried forward by controlled activity between manager and workforce, has the work of its disparate departments harmonized by coordinated management and, finally, is subject to checks on the efficiency of its working, preferably by independent 'staff' departments separate from the functional departments.

Fayol believed that a manager obtained the best performance from his workforce by leadership qualities, by his knowledge of the business and his workers, and by the ability to instil sense of mission. From his own long experience in industry, he distilled his fourteen General Principles of Management:

1. Division of work with specialization allowing individuals to build up skills and become more productive. 'The object of division of work is to produce more and better work with the same effort.'
2. Authority, both official and personal, with matching responsibility. 'Generally speaking, responsibility is feared as much as authority is sought after, and fear of

51

responsibility paralyses much initiative and destroys many good qualities. A good leader should possess and infuse into those around him courage to accept responsibility.'

3. Discipline, 'in essence obedience, application, energy, behaviour and outward marks of respect observed in accordance with the standing agreements between the firm and its employees . . . When a defect in discipline is apparent or when relations between superiors and subordinates leave much to be desired . . . the ill mostly results from the ineptitude of the leaders.'

4. Unity of command: each man should have only one boss with no conflicting lines of command. 'In all human associations, in industry, commerce, army, home, State, dual command is a perpetual source of conflicts . . .'

5. Unity of direction: 'one head and one plan for a group of activities having the same objective. It is the condition essential to unity of action, coordination of strength and focusing of effort.'

6. Subordination of individual to general interest, reconciling conflicting interests where necessary: 'That represents one of the great difficulties of management.' Means of effecting it are (1) firmness and good example on the part of superiors (2) agreements as fair as possible (3) constant supervision.

7. Fair remuneration for effort. 'Every mode of payment likely to make the personnel more valuable and improve its lot in life, and also to inspire keenness on the part of employees at all levels, should be a matter for managers' constant attention.'

8. Centralization or decentralization, the choice to depend on the condition of the business and the culture of its staff. 'The finding of the measure which shall give the best overall yield; that is the problem of centralisation or decentralisation. Everything which goes to increase the importance of the subordinate's role is decentralisation, everything which goes to reduce it is centralisation.'

9. The scalar chain or hierarchical principle of manage-

ment; a path 'dictated both by the need for some transmission and by the principle of unity of command, but it is not always the swiftest . . . It is an error to depart needlessly from the line of authority but an even greater one to keep to it when detriment to the business ensues . . . When an employee is obliged to choose between the two practices, and it is impossible for him to take advice from his superiors, he should be courageous enough and feel free enough to adopt the line dictated by the general interest.'

10. Order, both material and social: 'Social order demands precise knowledge of the human requirements and resources of the concern and a constant balance between these.'

11. Equity in the treatment of employees: 'the head of the business should strive to instil a sense of equity throughout all levels of the scalar chain.'

12. Stability of tenure among personnel: 'Generally the managerial personnel of prosperous concerns is stable, that of unsuccessful ones is unstable. Instability of tenure is at one and the same time cause and effect of bad running. Nevertheless, changes of personnel are inevitable . . . stability of tenure of personnel is also a question of proportion.'

13. Initiative: 'Thinking out a plan and ensuring its success is one of the keenest satisfactions for an intelligent man to experience. It is also one of the most powerful stimulants of human endeavour . . . The initiative of all, added to that of the manager and supplementing it if need be, represents a great source of strength for business . . . The manager must be able to sacrifice some personal vanity in order to grant this sort of satisfaction to subordinates.'

14. A sense of *esprit de corps*: essential for management to foster the morale of its workforce. 'Real talent is needed,' said Fayol, 'to coordinate effort, encourage keenness, use each person's abilities, and reward each one's merit without arousing possible jealousies and disturbing harmonious relations.'

KEY BOOKS

H. Fayol, trans. Constance Storrs (1949) *General and Industrial Management*, London: Pitman.
Quotations taken from extract in *Organization Theory* (1990) ed. D. S. Pugh, London: Penguin Books.

11

CHARLES HANDY

(b.1932)

The future of work and organizations

Britain's best-known contemporary business guru, noted for his studies of organizations and his far-reaching ideas on the future of work and business structures. Handy was born in Kildare into what he calls 'the Parnellian tradition,' the son of a southern Irish Protestant clergyman, and says this background is an important key to his development: 'it gave me a slightly irreverent streak and a tendency to ask 'why'?'

After graduating from Oriel College, Oxford, with a First in Greats, Handy worked for Shell International in Malaysia and as an economist in the City of London and then spent a formative two years at MIT's Sloan School of Management. Here he 'sat at the feet' of Warren Bennis (qv), an authority on organization theory but now principally associated with leadership, who remains a good friend and is probably his strongest influence ('Bennis is my godfather'); Ed Schein (qv), the 'career anchor' guru who became identified with the study of corporate culture; and Chris Argyris (qv), the organizational psychologist. Douglas McGregor, of Theory X and Y fame, had recently died, but his ideas still powerfully influenced a group of disciples at MIT.

Handy has said that his experiences working with the Sloan School gurus 'transformed my life.' It was the end of his fledgling career as a businessman; he returned to

London to launch and direct the Sloan Management Programme at the newly established London Business School, where he is still visiting professor of management, teaching managerial psychology and development.

From 1977 to 1981 he was Warden of St. George's House in Windsor Castle, a private conference and study centre concerned with issues of ethics and values in society. It was here that he carried out the research for *The Future of Work* (1984), and the appointment marked something of a watershed in his life. Handy went to St. George's instead of joining the church itself, and it enabled him to extend his teaching and thinking beyond business executives and management issues.

Handy's first book, *Understanding Organizations* (1976), has become a bible in some quarters and was revised for the second time in 1991 to take account of the vast changes in business cultures that have taken place since the mid-1970s.

His second book, *Gods of Management* (1978), which explored corporate culture in a highly original manner, is his personal favourite: he feels it is his most creative. 'It was before its time,' he says. 'It's still the best way of getting a quick fix on organizations and to find clues on how they need to change.'

It develops an apparently whimsical concept (first sketched out in *Understanding Organizations*) – that all organizations can be classified according to the characteristics of four ancient Greek gods: Zeus (power, patriarchy, the club culture); Apollo (order, reason and bureaucracy, the role culture); Athena (expertise, wisdom, meritocracy, the task culture); and Dionysus (individualism, professional rather than corporate, the existential culture). It is one of the earliest, though underrated, works on company culture.

In the 1980s, Handy turned away from full-time academic work, combining writing and broadcasting with teaching, and thus practising his own blueprint for 'portfolio' living as developed in *The Future of Work*. This stimulating volume threw off scores of ideas around the proposition that lifetime careers are becoming a thing of the past and that those fortunate individuals who are knowledge or brain workers rather than manual workers will in future be able to design a range of jobs for themselves to suit the way they want to spend their time.

The idea had already been touched upon in *Gods of Management* (each of Handy's books in a sense foreshadows the next), and is further elaborated in *The Age of Unreason* (1989, paperback 1990), which Handy regards as his most popular book, vividly encapsulating his principal theories on the implications of change in work and society. It is also the only one of his books to date to have been published in the United States, and so impressed Robert Horton, chairman and chief executive of British Petroleum, that he invited Handy to advise the company as a consultant.

Handy's joint study with John Constable of the state of management education, entitled *The Making of Managers* (1988), crystallized a widespread unease about the UK's persistent amateurism and accentuated the need to professionalize management. It led to formation of the Management Charter Initiative, in which several eminent management and professional bodies participated, though the concept of the 'chartered manager' has since become bogged down in arguments over qualifications. Handy's commitment to developing the right calibre of management is directly connected to his belief that managers in the future will no longer be able to rely on the experience of their predecessors to help them make decisions.

'Leaders of tomorrow's businesses will have to be more resourceful and imaginative to enable their businesses to survive,' as an article in *Director* summed it up in September, 1989, shortly before Handy began a bimonthly column for the magazine.

Handy is now veering into non-managerial fields of study, and concerning himself with ethics, values and corporate issues beyond the bottom line. Having broadcast regularly for four years in the BBC's radio 'God-slot', Thought for the Day, he published an anthology of these philosophical reflections under the title of *Waiting for the*

Mountain to Move (1991).

The diversity of Handy's interests and activities is evident from his work for the Royal Society for the Encouragement of the Arts, Manufactures and Commerce, more commonly known as the Royal Society of Arts. He was chairman of the RSA 1988–1989 and subsequently vice-chairman.

Handy's latest management book, *Inside Organizations*, was tied in with a BBC television series in 1991. It offers 21 managerial concepts for application to business problems, and is aimed at first-time managers in all types of organizations. It is supremely accessible in its language, using metaphors and anecdotes rather than technical jargon.

Charles Handy openly aspires to be numbered among those who 'change the way the world behaves' and who 'affect the way in which managers think.' In this generation his own list of gurus who have achieved such a status would include Drucker, Deming, Bennis, Porter, Peters, Pascale and Mintzberg.

Like Peter Drucker, Handy's eclectic range of interests and wide-angle view of economic and social change make him hard to categorize as a management guru. Drucker has written more on the techniques of management and has nearly 30 years' start on Handy, but both share a curiosity about the directions of society and a gift for extrapolating future trends. (Drucker's *The Age of Discontinuity* did for the 1970s and 1980s what Handy's *The Age of Unreason* may do for the 1990s and early twenty-first century – foreshadow cataclysms of change in industry and economics.)

Certain Handy concepts have remained constant throughout his writing – the increasing shift from lifetime employment in a single company to 'portfolio' work, less secure but more fulfilling; the evolution of new organizational forms such as the 'shamrock' company (a core of essential staff flanked by contract specialists and part-time helpers) and the 'Triple I' (information, intelligence, ideas), in which managers will be required to rise to the challenge of managing knowledge workers, individuals with far different aspirations from the hierarchy-conscious personnel of the past.

Increasingly, he is concerned with how companies manage their goals beyond the pursuit of profit, and whether they can develop into communities of human endeavour rather than properties to be bought and sold in the marketplace. He fears, however, that the Western model of company-as-property will prevail over the Eastern model of company-as-community.

For the student of management, business and the organizations that sustain them, Handy's *Understanding Organizations* provides a valuable synthesis of ideas propounded by himself and others. Here you will find explained the major theories of motivation and why we work – the satisfaction theory of Herzberg, the incentive theory of Morse and Weiss, the intrinsic theory of McGregor and Likert (the response of the individual to a worthwhile job).

The book also examines leadership and the culture of organizations, how people behave within them and the power games they play. Handy concludes with a preliminary sketch for his vision of the future organization, which has occupied much of his thinking since, including the changes wrought by communications (fewer people needing to travel physically to their place of work) and leaner organizations paying fees to contract workers rather than salaries and overheads to staff.

Handy says he writes books to clarify his ideas and advises readers of *Understanding Organizations* to 'burn this book after reading it and to write their own – it's the only way to really own the concepts.' It is not, he emphasizes, a book purely for students of business, but concerns organizations of all kinds. He has written separately on schools as organizations and on voluntary organizations.

'Organizations are changing,' he told an interviewer in *Director* magazine in September 1989. 'The days have gone when you went into the kitchens and worked your way up. Soon there won't be promotion prospects after 30. People have got to be prepared to run their own operations – to be competent in all aspects of management.' As the monolithic 'palace' structures of corporations give way, he says memorably, 'we are being thrust into a world of tents.'

In *The Age of Unreason* (his name for the coming era of wrenching change), Handy warns that in the business organization, as in other areas of life, 'the status quo will no longer be the best way forward.' To counter the challenge, he recommends a process he calls 'upside-down thinking,' a process not unrelated to Edward de Bono's (qv) 'lateral thinking.' The book shows how the technique can be applied to solving problems of change and, though written for a popular readership, offers stimulating new perspectives to managers and students of management.

KEY BOOKS

Handy, C. (1976) *Understanding Organizations*, London: Penguin Books.

Handy C. (1986, 1991) *Gods of Management*, London: Souvenir Press; Business Books.

Handy, C. (1984, 1986) *The Future of Work*, Oxford: Basil Blackwell.

Handy, C. and Constable, J. (1988) *The Making of Managers*, London: Longman.

Handy, C. (1989, 1990) *The Age of Unreason*, London: Business Books; Arrow.

Handy, C. (1990) *Inside Organizations: 21 Ideas for Managers*, London: BBC Books.

12

FREDERICK HERZBERG

(b.1923)

'Motivation' and 'maintenance' factors in job satisfaction

US clinical psychologist, now professor of management at the University of Utah, whose work on human motivation separates the elements of a job into those serving animal or economic needs ('hygiene' or 'maintenance' factors) and those meeting deeper aspirations ('motivation' factors). Herzberg gives these a timeless context with Biblical analogies and believes that individual needs and expectations 'are shaped by the religious/philosophical system in which one lives.'

More urgently, he relates job satisfaction or dissatisfaction to mental health, and has described his work as originating in his World War II experiences as a US army volunteer posted to Dachau concentration camp after liberation. Here, he 'realised that a society goes insane when the sane are driven insane.' After the war, he worked for the US Public Health Service on research projects, particularly concerning mental illness. Reading all that had been published on industrial psychology up to that time, he identified a void in conceptual thinking that he set out to fill with his behavioural theories.

Herzberg, who coined the concept of 'job enrichment' to add motivational factors (he says the theory has 'given employment to a hell of a lot of consultants'), is also one of the few management thinkers and writers to have worked at the sharp end of industry as a consultant; in his case, with the telecommunications giant AT&T. He distilled his thinking about motivation in a 1968 *Harvard Business Review* article – 'One More Time: How Do You Motivate Employees?' which is said to be that journal's biggest selling article, with well over a million reprinted copies sold.

It was Herzberg's 1959 book *The Motivation to Work*, written in collaboration with two research colleagues, B. Mausner and B. B. Snyderman, that established him as an original thinker about the mainsprings of human activity in the workplace. The type of investigation it used has been followed by at least 16 other studies, some in Communist countries, making the original research, in Herzberg's words, 'one of the most replicated studies in the field of job attitudes.'

The Motivation to Work was based on intensive questioning of 200 Pittsburgh engineers and accountants, asking them to analyse times when they felt exceptionally good and exceptionally bad about their work. The book was the first to discover that satisfaction and dissatisfaction with one's employment arose from quite different factors and were not simply opposing reactions to the same factors.

The factors that led to feelings of satisfaction, Herzberg found, were 'motivation' ones such as achievement, recognition, satisfaction in the nature of the work itself, responsibility, progress and personal growth (of which the last three were the most important). Dissatisfaction nearly always related to 'hygiene' factors such as company policy, working conditions, salary, status and job security.

'Man has two sets of needs,' explained Herzberg in a later book, *Work and the Nature of Man*; 'his need as an animal to avoid pain and his need as a human to grow psychologically.'

Herzberg illustrates his theory by Biblical example. 'Motivation' is represented by Abraham, made in the image of God and capable of great achievements in self-development; 'hygiene' by Adam, who was faced after the expulsion from Eden with the need to meet bodily requirements – food, warmth, safety, security, avoidance of pain. Both are part of the human condition at work, argues Herzberg, and a lack in one cannot be compensated by fulfilment in the other. 'Animal-Adam' seeks avoidance of pain from the environment or job; 'Human-Abraham' seeks growth and self-realization from tasks. The individual becomes unhappy without the first factor, but it brings only temporary relief, like an analgesic, and the effects soon wear off without deeper satisfactions.

Herzberg's solution was to evolve an 'industrial engineering' philosophy which would design the 'Abraham' factor into jobs. This technique he called 'job enrichment.'

Where it has been done – for example, by enhancing a worker's accountability or by giving him or her additional authority – the changes have brought substantial benefits.

As jobs become 'enriched,' the need for much mundane job supervision disappears, and hitherto unsatisfying supervisory tasks can themselves be enriched by enlarging their responsibilities on a more managerial level.

Herzberg's motivation theories have been reflected in many recent corporate developments such as 'flexitime' and the 'cafeteria' system of choice within a company's benefits system.

KEY BOOKS

Herzberg, F; Mausner, B: Snyderman, B. (1959) *The Motivation to Work*, New York: Wiley.

Herzberg, F. (1966) *Work and the Nature of Man*, World Publishing.

Herzberg, F. (1968) 'One More Time: How Do You Motivate Employees?' in *Harvard Business Review*, Cambridge, Mass.

Herzberg, F. (1976) *Managerial Choice: To be Efficient and to be Human*, Dow Jones, Irwin.

13

JOHN HUMBLE

(b. 1925)

Management By Objectives as a practical methodology

British management consultant who took Peter Drucker's concept of Management By Objectives and developed it as a practical tool for managers.

Humble, a Cambridge graduate, is a former director of the old-established consultancy Urwick Orr, whose founder Lyndall Urwick introduced scientific management principles to Britain in the 1920s. Humble has been at the forefront of management development in the UK for many years. In 1967 he joined the Central Training Council of the Department of Employment and later served on the management education committee of the National Economic Development Council. He has also headed consulting teams in many sectors of industry from engineering to retail distribution.

Humble has written or edited half a dozen books. In 1966 he received the British Institute of Management's Burnham Medal 'in recognition of his original work in the area of management objectives.'

The theory of Management By Objectives (MBO) was conceived by Peter Drucker in the 1950s to define the tasks required of the visionary manager, the manager who can see the goals of the business beyond his functional role. Drucker identified eight areas in a business that were suitable for performance objectives: market standing, innovation, productivity, physical and financial resources, profitability, manager performance and development, worker performance and attitude, and public responsibility. Managers also needed, he said, to devise a measuring system for their objectives and a realistic time scale for their achievement.

Every manager from the chairman to the chief clerk needs 'clearly spelled out objectives,' said Drucker. These objectives should set out what each manager's unit is expected to achieve, with the emphasis on teamwork: other units cooperate towards the manager's goals, while his unit in turn helps others to achieve theirs.

'These objectives should always derive from the goals of the business enterprise' and managers needed to be able to measure their performance against these goals, said Drucker.

Drucker called MBO 'a philosophy of management,' John Humble was the first to introduce it to the UK and to develop the philosophy into a practical methodology. He spent three months in the US on a Ford Foundation grant studying best practice in American companies.

Humble defined MBO as 'the attempt to clarify the goals of management objectivity so that the responsibility for achieving the goals was reasonably distributed round the management team, and to check standards of performance against which management effectiveness can be measured.'

The idea of breaking down corporate aims into a series of personal objectives throughout the management team sounds simple but runs the risk of the objectives being too ambitious or too modest to work. Many companies subsequently suffered from too rigid a faith in planning and forecasting and the temptation to pitch their objectives too high without, in the words of a Beecham Group executive, 'legislating for failure.' The reverse danger, of setting objectives too low, tended to be overlooked in Humble's elegant circular structure that moved from strategic planning to tactical planning to unit planning to individual managers' results and back to review, control and strategic planning.

Humble intended to encourage managers throughout the organization to play 'a creative part' in establishing the standards of performance they would be expected to meet, a sort of continuous self-appraisal mechanism working for the corporate good, and at the same time enhancing personal satisfaction. But, as management writer Robert Heller has pointed out: 'The executive soon catches on to the notion that, if he is being held to a plan or objective, the plan had better be one he can meet.'

MBO in its original form has few adherents today, though elements have been adopted by most successful businesses and strategic planning in particular has an increasingly recognized role in British corporations.

Humble later switched the focus of his work to studying the impact and integration of information technology on business strategy, and in the 1970s concentrated on the often controversial role of the multinational corporation and its responsibilities to the communities in which it operates, particularly in the Third World.

KEY BOOK

Humble, J. W. (1971) *Management By Objectives*, Maidenhead: McGraw-Hill.

14

ELLIOTT JAQUES

(b.1917)

Psychological and social factors in group behaviour

Canadian psychologist and doctor of medicine who became a founder member of the Tavistock Institute of Human Relations in London, an organization that did much pioneering work after World War II on the sociology of industry and management. A graduate of both the University of Toronto (BA and MA) and Johns Hopkins Medical School (MD), Jaques served as a major in the Royal Canadian Army Medical Corps between 1941 and 1945.

Jaques's principal fame rests on his work in studying the psychological and social factors behind group behaviour, first carried out at the Glacier Metal Company in London. He also developed a theory of measuring the value of work by the time span of 'discretion' that elapses before decisions are monitored.

Since the mid-1960s Jaques has been associated with Brunel University in Uxbridge, Middlesex, as head of the School of Social Science (1965–70) and director of the university's Institute of Organisation and Social Studies (1970–85). He has been a government adviser to the Board of Trade on overseas marketing and on the reorganization of the National Health Service. Jaques retired from Brunel in 1985 and is now visiting professor of management science at George Washington University, Washington, D.C.

Elliott Jaques's studies in worker behaviour at the Glacier Metal Company, carried out between 1948 and 1965, were at least a decade ahead of their time and remain the most extensive of their kind to be carried out on the factory floor. The 'working-through' process he pioneered, using an investigator interacting with a group on its problems, uncovered, most importantly, the need that workpeople feel to have their role and status defined in a way that they and their colleagues can accept. Confusion of roles or unclear boundaries of responsibility lead to frustration and insecurity, and to a tendency in management to avoid authority and accountability.

Jaques's work on wage problems at Glacier Metal led to him formulating a theory of the value of different types of work, based on 'the time-span of discretion' – the length of time that elapses before the actions or decision of an individual worker are monitored by superiors. The lowest-paid workers tend to have their actions monitored at frequent intervals, whereas high-level decisions may take years to be evaluated. This resulted in a book called *The Measurement of Responsibility* in 1956, five years after his ground-breaking Glacier investigations were published as *The Changing Culture of a Factory*. (Jaques also collaborated with the managing director of Glacier Metal, Wilfred Brown, on the *Glacier Project Papers* in 1965.)

Jaques later developed a theory of bureaucracy in which progression up an organization, with increasing levels of discretion, was not viewed in relation to a simple chronological time-span, but as seven main strata defined by length of service: up to three months; up to one year; two years; five years; ten years, 20 years and more than 20 years. These were the levels at which pay differentials were accepted as being fair. Jaques maintains that any rational pay policy would be accepted as just if differences between these discretionary levels were properly worked out first.

In *A General Theory of Bureaucracy*, Jaques also examines the different perceptions of a worker when asked to describe his boss. He may see his 'real' boss – the one from whom he feels he has a chance of getting a decision about himself – as someone quite different from the person next in line up the hierarchy.

Jaques quotes from military staff example to illustrate that real decisions are never made in the way they are supposed to be made in the hierarchy charts. 'They would all be killed while trying to sort out who was giving orders to whom.' He concludes from this and bureaucratic example in Eastern Europe (of the 1970s) 'that it is never possible to tell from an organisation chart just who is manager of whom: in effect, it is a wise manager (or subordinate) who knows his own subordinate (or manager).'*

KEY BOOKS

Jaques, E: (1951) *The Changing Culture of a Factory*, London: Tavistock.

Jaques, E. (1956) *The Measurement of Responsibility*, London: Tavistock.

Brown, W. and Jaques, E. (1965) *Glacier Project Papers*, London: Heinemann.

Jaques, E. (1961, 1967) *Equitable Payment*, London: Heinemann; Penguin Books.

Jaques, E. (1976) *A General Theory of Bureaucracy*, London: Heinemann.

Jaques, E. (1982) *Free Enterprise, Fair Employment*, London: Hienemann.

*E. Jaques. *A General Theory of Bureaucracy* (Heinemann, 1976), quoted in *Organization Theory*, ed D. S. Pugh (Penguin, 1990)

15

JOSEPH M. JURAN

(b.1904)

Company-wide quality cannot be delegated

US electrical engineer, born in Romania, who worked contemporaneously with W. Edwards Deming (qv) on pioneering the quality management revolution that began in postwar Japan. Ironically, no industrialist in the US was interested in the theories of Deming and Juran – the production mentality ruled at the time – until Japanese manufacturing, practising the quality philosophy, began driving American products to the wall.

By coincidence, both Deming and Juran had become interested in the techniques of assuring quality in manufacturing based on statistical control while working in the 1920s at Western Electric, the manufacturing division of Bell Telephone System. Juran joined Western in 1924, three years before the famous Elton Mayo (qv) experiments at Western's Hawthorne plant in Chicago, which revolutionized thinking about motivation and the human element in industry.

Juran then joined the manufacturing side of AT&T in the 1920s. He became a corporate industrial engineer and later branched out as a quality consultant.

Juran established his reputation in 1951 with the publication of his *Quality Control Handbook*, the first manual of its kind. The Japanese, who had already absorbed Deming's lessons to the extent of instituting a Deming Prize that year, invited Juran to Tokyo in 1953 for a series of lectures. In the early 1980s his contribution to Japanese quality achievements was recognized with the award of the Order of the Sacred Treasure, second class, an honour also conferred on Deming.

Since 1954 he has preached his gospel in Japan and claims some of the credit for turning round Japan's initially poor reputation for quality. His 'Management of Quality' courses have been attended by more than 20,000 managers in over 30 countries. As a consultant, his clients include Texas Instruments, Du Pont, Monsanto, Xero, Motorola and the Internal Revenue Service.

Juran's principal contribution to quality management thinking is his methodology for determining the avoidable and the unavoidable costs of quality, thus providing a yardstick for measuring the cost of a quality programme.

Juran has devised a structured concept known as CWQM – Company-Wide Quality Management. He believes it absolutely essential for senior managers to involve themselves, to define the goals, to assign responsibilities and to measure progress. Quality, Juran teaches, cannot be delegated.

Like other management thinkers – notably Peter Drucker (qv), Charles Handy (qv) and Rosabeth Moss Kanter (qv) – Juran has developed a vision of the future corporation, in which he sees quality targets being incorporated in business plans as routinely as targets for sales, profits, return on capital and earnings per share. Like Moss Kanter, Juran sees greater 'empowerment' of the workforce as a key – in this case to achieving quality through self-organization and self-supervision. For Juran, quality has always been indissolubly linked with human relations and teamwork.

Joseph M. Juran and W. Edwards Deming are so closely linked – by age, experience and their part in the Japanese economic miracle – that it is sometimes hard to differentiate their contributions. Juran himself has set out to develop Company-Wide Quality Management into a full-blown corporate philosophy, and has criticized the Deming approach for being more at home with statistics than with management.

Juran's approach is heavily oriented towards the human side of achieving quality, and he has praised the Japanese use of quality circles for their effect on human relations in the workplace, while acknowledging that QCs have accounted for less than ten per cent of Japan's improvement in quality.

The Juran methodology has most recently been laid out in *Juran on Planning for Quality* (1988), which sets out to demonstrate how quality planning affects different levels of company activity. It outlines the Juran 'quality trilogy' – quality planning, quality management and quality improvement – by which managers learn how to implement strategic quality planning across the company.

Key elements include: identifying customers and their needs; creating measurements of quality; planning processes that are capable of meeting quality goals under operating conditions; producing continuing improvements in market share and premium prices and in reducing the error rate.

The book emphasizes the universal application of quality commitment throughout an organization – to all products, both goods and services; to all corporate levels from CEO downwards; to all corporate functions from general management to product development; and to all industries, in both the manufacturing and service sectors.

KEY BOOKS

Juran, J. M. (1951) *Quality Control Handbook*,
Juran, J. M. (1988) *Juran on Planning for Quality*, New York: Free Press; London: Collier Macmillan.

16

ROSABETH MOSS KANTER

(b.1943)

The 'post-entrepreneurial' corporation;
empowering individuals as a force for change

US sociologist, currently professor of business administration at Harvard and editor of the *Harvard Business Review*, who has established herself as a leading authority on managing change, developing the 'post-entrepreneurial' corporation and 'empowering' human potential in organizations. She is now one of the most sought-after consultants in the US (clients include IBM, CBS, Procter & Gamble, Honeywell, Digital, Apple, Xerox and General Electric) and a celebrated TV performer on both sides of the Atlantic. A BBC television documentary described her as 'a fearless critic of management tradition.'

Born in Cleveland, Ohio, Moss Kanter graduated from the élite female academy Bryn Mawr and took her Ph.D. at the University of Michigan, later joining the faculty of Brandeis University as associate professor of sociology before moving to Harvard in 1973. Between 1977 and 1986 she taught at Yale and MIT before returning to Harvard as professor of business administration. In 1988 she worked as a key economic adviser to Michael Dukakis in his campaign for the Presidency against George Bush.

Kanter's award-winning first book, *Men and Women of the Corporation* (1977) analysed the bureaucratic factors that locked people into pre-determined roles in a code-named industrial corporation, and how this prevented the business from fully tapping the talent within it.

The Change Masters (1983) compared the characteristics of such change-resisters with those of innovative corporations which stimulated entrepreneurship within themselves and became market leaders. Combining as it did the academic discipline of Kanter's background in organizational sociology with her hands-on experience as a consultant in industry, the book was hailed as 'the thinking manager's *In Search of Excellence.*'

When Giants Learn to Dance (1989) in effect completed a trilogy on the deep changes facing corporate America. Kanter examined a broad range of corporations, large and small, working from the inside on consulting projects, and found that very different organizations were converging towards similar solutions to the problems of competing in the new global 'corporate Olympics.'

The new model corporation Kanter outlines for the 1990s is 'post-entrepreneurial' – lean and athletic with fewer management levels, able to 'do more with less,' to anticipate change and open itself up to opportunities such as strategic alliances with other companies. A focal point of the corporate Olympic runner is to achieve synergies, where the whole is worth more than the sum of its parts; Kanter's inside studies of merger and acquisition strategy and culture change are particularly fascinating.

The last third of the book studies the impact of the post-entrepreneurial organization on the people who work in it. The implications for careers (from climbing the corporate ladder to developing portable 'employability'), for pay (as determinants switch from position to performance, from status to contribution), and for the psychological wellbeing of individuals are all explored with stimulating intellectual zeal. The trilogy thus in a sense comes full circle, focusing on the key task of managing the creative potential of the men and women of the corporation as corporate reality changes about them.

The book achieved both intellectual and popular status within a short time: Tom Peters has described it as 'the benchmark against which management books of the nineties are measured.'

Rosabeth Moss Kanter has pursued a logical progression from studying how traditional, bureaucratic organizations stultify individual talents to identifying how the 'post-entrepreneurial' corporation is releasing and 'empowering' those talents in flatter, less hierarchical structures.

Men and Women of the Corporation, which won a US award in 1977 for the best book on social issues, discovered that the highest value placed on managers was 'predictability.' Women, whether in the traditional roles of secretaries or company wives (with all their potential for influence in the corporation) were regarded as both unpredictable and incomprehensible.

Kanter's research for this book led her to conclude that there was crucial need for change in the average industrial corporation in order to improve the quality of working life, to create equal employment opportunities for men, women and minority groups, and to enable employees to make better use of their talents to the benefit of the corporation. To achieve this, she perceived that the following changes in organizational structure would be required:

1. Management should be opened up to promotion from a wider range of candidates, including women and hitherto powerless individuals like clerical workers. Changes in certain areas, such as systems of appraisal and career development, would be needed to achieve this. Intermediate jobs would need to be created to bridge these jobs with management.
2. Empowering strategies would be necessary, leading to a flatter hierarchy, decentralized authority and autonomous work groups.

Building on her discoveries about resistance to change, Kanter's second book studied in depth leading companies that could be defined as 'change masters,' illuminating the factors that encourage innovation as a way of life, and the problems that the search for innovation brings in its wake. Kanter's principal discovery was that firms prone to innovate have an 'integrative' approach to problems and a willingness to challenge established practices; to judge a course of action by a vision of the future rather than by the accepted ways of the past. Firms unlikely to innovate were typically 'segmentalist' in approach, compartmented by department and unable to see problems whole.

Throughout *The Change Masters*, Kanter argued that the key to a corporate renaissance was 'participation management' or empowerment – making possible the mechanisms by which individuals could contribute their ideas. It is only in integrative companies that individuals can improve their leverage, thus contributing to their own and the corporate success.

When Giants Learn to Dance (1989) extends this philosophy to the future shape and character of the globally competitive corporation, which she describes as 'post-entrepreneurial . . . applying entrepreneurial principles to the giant corporation' in order to make it flexible and responsive to change while maintaining a disciplined efficiency – combining 'the power of an elephant with the agility of a dancer.' In the aftermath of the 'excellence' era, she suggests, companies are facing some problems not addressed by Peters and Waterman, such as 'Who has the power to start or block innovations?' and 'Who gets the financial returns?'

Kanter's detailed and knowledgeable case studies suggest that companies as different as, for example, Eastman Kodak and Apple Computers, are increasingly converging towards similar solutions when faced with the challenge of competing in the global 'corporate Olympics.' Her practical experience as a consultant comes through in such examples of the new strategy as 'the corporation as switchboard', where comparatively small head offices manage a network of other organizations, or contract out former company services as market-oriented businesses. (A crucial by-product of the latter, essential to Kanter's argument, is that staffs are no longer considered as 'overhead' but as potential sources of value.)

Much of the book is devoted to the study of achieving

synergy and all the components required for it, including the flatter management structure which enables greater cooperation across divisions and departments.

Another key idea is encapsulated in the acronym PAL – '*pool* resources with others, *ally* to exploit an opportunity or *link* systems in a partnership.' Companies can become better PALs with suppliers, venture partners, service contractors, customers and unions. In purchasing, for example, they shed the adversarial character of earlier practice, when the prevailing wisdom was to minimize price by maintaining a large vendor base and insisting on short-term contracts. The growth of joint ventures as a means of access to foreign markets has contributed strongly to the new ethos.

Kanter's keen perception of the individual human dimension within organizations leads her to identify the dangers in becoming more 'mean' than 'lean' and to stress, on a personal level, the importance of shared values in the corporation.

The impact of post-entrepreneurialism on individual careers, with rewards linked more to contribution than to position or status, and with a more flexible structure bringing an end to the lifetime career ladder, is fully explored. Management, for its part, becomes even more complex and demanding when it switches from the mentality of boss to that of partner.

Empowering the individual within the company, which this implies, has been a Kanter preoccupation for years. In 1979, her *Harvard Business Review* article 'Power Failures in Management Circuits' (HBR July/August 1979) identified those organizational factors affecting individuals which create power or powerlessness to influence events and people, e.g. discretion, recognition, relevance to central problems, sponsors, peer networks and subordinates.

'The powerless live in a different world . . . they may turn instead to the ultimate weapon of those who lack productive power – oppressive power . . . .' This she identified as a prime cause of dissatisfaction with frontline supervisors, a category especially subject to the feeling of powerlessness. Staff professionals and isolated top executives are other susceptible categories, leading in Kanter's view to conservatism and resistance to change in those areas. Women managers experience particular failures of power, she found, because organizations are geared to employing them in routine, low-profile jobs.

Kanter's key message here is: 'By empowering others, a leader does not decrease his power; instead, he may increase it – especially if the whole organization performs better.'

Her seven essential skills for managers of the future, set out in *When Giants Learn to Dance*, are:

- learn to operate without the hierarchy 'crutch'
- know how to compete in a way that enhances, not undercuts, co-operation
- operate to the highest ethical standards
- possess a dose of humility
- develop a process focus on how things are done
- be multi-faceted and ambidextrous, work across functions to find synergies
- be able to gain satisfaction from results and be willing to stake your own rewards on them.

Kanter's post-entrepreneurial model corporation is a three-part mix: the values and goals emanating from top management; the channels, forums, programmes and relationships designed in the middle to support those goals and values; and the project ideas bubbling up from below – 'ideas for new ventures or technological innovations, or better ways to serve customers.'

Her books deserve careful and thoughtful reading: their many-faceted ideas resist easy categorization and will play a shaping role in management theory for years to come.

KEY BOOKS

Kanter, R. M. (1977) *Men and Women of the Corporation*, Basic Books.

Kanter, R. M. (1983, 1984) *The Change Masters: Corporate Entrepreneurs at Work*, New York: Simon and Schuster; London: Allen & Unwin.

Kanter, R. M. (1989) *When Giants Learn to Dance*, New York and London: Simon & Schuster.

Kanter, R. M. (1979) 'Power Failures in Management Circuits', Cambridge, Mass: *Harvard Business Review*; reprinted in *Organization Theory*, (1990) ed. D. S. Pugh, London: Penguin Books.

17

THEODORE LEVITT

(b.1925)

Marketing as a key to successful business management

The first management theorist to emphasize the importance of marketing, German-born Levitt, who has been
associated with Harvard Business School for over thirty
years, is unusual in having established his reputation as
a guru on the basis of a single article – 'Marketing
Myopia', published in the *Harvard Business Review* in
the summer of 1960. It has since sold more than 500,000
reprinted copies.

In this extraordinarily influential article, Levitt argued
powerfully that 'an industry is a customer-satisfying
process, not a goods-producing process.' He suggested,
for example, that railway managers helped to cause
problems in their industry by viewing their business as
railways, a technical product, rather than transport, a
customer business. This was the approach reversed by
Lord King and Sir Colin Marshall at British Airways, and
which led to a dramatic turnround in the airline's
performance and in the perception of it by its customers.
Before Levitt, it has been said, marketing was a poor
relation in the world of senior management. Levitt can
claim to have had more articles published in the *Harvard
Business Review* than any other guru. He edited the
journal from 1986 to 1990, when he was succeeded by
Rosabeth Moss Kanter. Of his five books on marketing,
he regards *The Marketing Imagination* (1983) as his most

important. He believes the secret of success in marketing is constantly to 'ask questions to develop your sensitivity and sensibility . . . perceptiveness requires cognitive effort and personal involvement. You bring something to what you see.'

Like other gurus, notably Kenichi Ohmae, Levitt has recently diversified into the subject of the global market-place and 'global branding.' Selling the same product worldwide, whether baked beans or cameras, is a subject of divided opinions among gurus; Ohmae, for example, taking the view that acting as an 'insider' in the territory you are selling in is more important than selling a standard product from a central point, whereas Levitt inclines to the latter view.

Levitt's view of his own influence is modest. 'What I've achieved, I think, is to make myself effective in some way, kept myself intellectually curious, alive and productive, and made myself interesting to myself.' (*Makers of Management:* Clutterbuck and Crainer)

Theodore Levitt's ground-breaking article 'Marketing Myopia' started by pointing out that every industry was once a growth industry. After growth continues for a while, managers tend to believe it will always do so. Seeing no competition for their product, they pin their faith on improvements in productivity and cost reduction. The result is stagnation or decline.

Levitt proceeds to demonstrate that only 'a thoroughly customer-oriented management' can keep a growth industry growing 'even after the obvious opportunities have been exhausted'.

Detroit's automobile industry provided a key case study for Levitt's thesis. Ruled by the production ('Fordist') philosophy, it went on giving the customer what it believed the customer should have. 'Detroit never really researched the customer's wants,' wrote Levitt. 'It only researched the kinds of things which it had already decided to offer him.'

It was not until Japanese and European manufacturers won huge sales with compact cars that Detroit woke up to the reality of a shift in its traditional customer base.

Other long-successful industries, Levitt suggested, could be overtaken by the same nemesis unless they reversed the habits of an organizational lifetime and realized that 'an industry begins with the customer and his needs, not with a patent, a raw material, or a selling skill.'

Selling, Levitt insisted, was not the same as marketing. 'Selling concerns itself with the tricks and techniques of getting people to exchange their cash for your product. It is not concerned with the values that the exchange is all about. And it does not, as marketing invariably does, view the entire business process as consisting of a tightly integrated effort to discover, create, arouse and satisfy customer needs.'

The difference between marketing and selling, Levitt continued, was 'more than semantic. Selling focuses on the needs of the seller, marketing on the needs of the buyer. Selling is preoccupied with the seller's need to convert his product into cash; marketing with the idea of satisfying the needs of the customer by means of the product and the whole cluster of things associated with creating, delivering and finally consuming it.'

In a truly marketing-oriented firm, says Levitt, what is offered for sale is much more than the basic product or service – how it is made available to the customer, for example, under what conditions and terms of trade. 'Most important, what it offers for sale is determined not by the seller but by the buyer . . . the product becomes a consequence of the marketing effort, not vice versa.'

Taking a deliberately bizarre example of an industry that could have prevented its demise by understanding the wants of its customers, Levitt cites the makers of buggy whips in the early days of the automobile. 'No amount of product improvement could stave off its death sentence. But had the industry defined itself as being in the transportation business rather than the buggy whip business, it might have survived. It would have done what survival always entails, that is, changing. Even if it had only defined its business as providing a stimulant or catalyst to an energy source, it

82

might have survived by becoming a manufacturer of, say, fanbelts or air cleaners.'

In *The Marketing Imagination*, Levitt argued that competitive success rested on realizing five factors:

1. The purpose of a business is to create and keep customers.
2. To do this, goods and services must be produced and delivered that people want and value, at prices and conditions that are more attractive than those of competitors.
3. To continue, enough profits must be made to keep investors.
4. To achieve this, all companies must clarify their purposes, strategies and plans, and clearly communicate them to the workforce. The larger the enterprise, the greater the need for a clearly written and reviewed set of goals.
5. All enterprises must have a system of rewards, audits and controls to ensure the proper pursuit of those goals.

The organization, Levitt constantly preaches, must think of itself less in terms of producing goods or services and more in terms of buying customers. To achieve this, the chief executive's leadership is all-important.

Today marketing is no longer, as Levitt called it in 1960, a 'stepchild.' Getting and staying close to the customer was enshrined by Tom Peters and Robert Waterman's *In Search of Excellence* as a prime component of the top-performing company. But that was in 1982. More than twenty years earlier, the idea was sufficiently novel for Levitt's *Harvard Business Review* article to start an earthquake in management thinking.

KEY BOOKS

Levitt, T. (1960) 'Marketing Myopia', Cambridge, Mass., *Harvard Business Review*.

Levitt, T. (1962) *Innovation in Marketing*, New York: McGraw-Hill.
Levitt, T. (1969) *The Marketing Mode*, New York: McGraw-Hill.
Levitt, T. (1983) *The Marketing Imagination*, New York: Free Press.

18

RENSIS LIKERT

(1903–1981)

How leadership styles link with business performance

US social psychologist and researcher who founded in 1949 a pioneering establishment for research into human behaviour in organizations, the Institute for Social Research at the University of Michigan. His work had a lasting effect on organizational theory and the study of leadership. He is best known for his *New Patterns of Management* (1961), in which, based on extensive questioning of employees in industrial firms, he argued that the management of organizations could be categorized along a line graduating from System 1, exploitative and authoritarian, to System 4, participative and based on overlapping work groups. He also invented the concept of 'linking plans' – individuals capable of linking each work group to the organization.

Like Douglas McGregor (qv), Likert rejected traditional assumptions about human behaviour under management and proposed new methods based on a better understanding of people's motivation and potential.

Likert gained a Ph.D. from Columbia University in 1932, and his work there was later published as 'A Technique for the Measurement of Attitudes.' He then became director of research at a life insurance office in Hartford, Connecticut, where he began to study management practices. In 1939 he moved to the Department of Agriculture in Washington as director of program surveys.

From 1949 to 1969 he ran the Institute for Social Research and on retirement formed his own consulting firm. His books are underpinned with numerous original research studies, the last of them being written with his wife and co-researcher, Jane Gibson Likert.

Rensis Likert believed that participative management was the best kind, and the most likely to produce results. Some of his contemporary management thinkers criticized him for flatly assuming that group discussion was the only way to good decision-making and thereby abandoning or ignoring the search for better techniques of problem-solving or decision-making.

Kepner and Tregoe in *The Rational Manager* (1965) commented that managers would find this both difficult and 'far removed from the practical reality they must contend with every day.'

Likert's primary objective at the Institute for Social Research was to identify different styles of leadership and correlate them with business performance. His research method was based on detailed questionnaires to employees of US companies, asking them a series of questions about their supervisors. He then drew up a profile of each supervisor or manager in the light of how he was viewed by the people who worked under him. From these profiles Likert established his System 1 to 4 progressive chart of management styles:

1. Exploitative authoritarian: management by fear and coercion, where communication is top-down, decision-making is done at the top with no shared processes, and superiors and subordinates are psychologically far apart.
2. Benevolent authoritarian: management by carrot rather than stick, but subordinates are still basically subservient; such information as flows upwards is mainly what the boss is thought to want to hear, and policy decisions are taken at the top, with only minor ones delegated to

a lower level.

3. Consultative: management uses both carrot and stick and does try to talk to employees; communication flows both ways but is still somewhat limited upwards; important decisions are still taken top-down.

4. Participative: management provides economic rewards and is concerned to get employees involved in groups capable of making decisions; it sets challenging goals and works closely with employees to encourage high performance. Communication flows easily in both directions and sideways to peers; superiors and subordinates are psychologically close. Decision-making is done through participative processes: work groups are integrated into the formal structure of the organization by creating a series of overlapping groups with each linked to the rest of the organization by a 'linking pin' – preferably a team leader or departmental manager, who will be a member of both group and management.

Likert's research suggested that departments which were low in efficiency tended to be in the charge of 'job-centred' supervisors; that is, Taylorist managers who keep their subordinates busily engaged in a 'specified work cycle in a prescribed way and at a satisfactory rate as determined by time standards.'

Supervisors with the best record of performance tended to be 'employee-centred,' to regard their chief task as dealing with people rather than work and who focused on building effective work groups that in turn were set high achievement goals. Such supervisors exercised general rather than detailed supervision of their subordinates and were more concerned with overall targets than with methods. They also allowed the maximum participation in decision-making.

In *New Ways of Managing Conflict*, Likert and his wife profile the System 4 Total Model Organization (System 4T), which adds certain characteristics to System 4, such as high levels of performance goals, transmitted by leader to subordinates; a high level of skill and knowledge on the part of the leader, and the leader's capacity to provide planning, resources, equipment and help for subordinates. System 4T is the optimum Likert structure in terms of linkages and group working relationships, and he conceives it as the best means of dealing with conflict in an organization.

Likert argues that the nearer an organization approaches to System 4T, the more its productivity and profitability will improve and conflict be reduced. Beyond this, he also suggests a System 5 for the future, in which all authority on a hierarchy basis will disappear, such authority as individuals retain deriving only from their 'linking pin' roles and the overlapping of groups.

The basic principle behind the work of both Likert and McGregor is that effective modern organizations must see themselves as interacting groups of people with supporting relationships to each other. The ideal goal is to achieve an organization in which the organization's objectives become of personal significance to everyone working in it. In pursuit of this, management must be a relative process, always adapting itself to the individual human beings who are led by it.

KEY BOOKS

Likert, R. (1961) *New Patterns of Management*, New York: McGraw-Hill.
Likert, R. (1967) *The Human Organization: Its Management and Value*, New York: McGraw-Hill.
Likert, R. and Likert, J. G. (1976) *New Ways of Managing Conflict*, New York: McGraw-Hill.

19

DOUGLAS McGREGOR

(1906–1964)

Theory X and Theory Y: authoritarian vs participative management

US social psychologist specializing in human behaviour within organizations, and famous for his formulation of 'Theory X' (authoritarian management) and 'Theory Y' (participative management), first propounded in his 1960 book *The Human Side of Enterprise*.

For some years president of Antioch College, McGregor was professor of management at the Massachusetts Institute of Technology from 1954 until his death in 1964.

McGregor shared many of his ideas on human wants with Abraham Maslow (qv) and Rensis Likert (qv). Maslow experimented with Theory Y in a California electronics plant and concluded that it did not wholly work in practice. Further work on motivating human achievement which revealed Theory Y as insufficiently flexible was done after McGregor's death by David C. McClelland of Harvard.

Douglas McGregor believed that the way an organization was run stemmed directly from the beliefs of its managers. 'Behind every managerial decision or action are assumptions about human nature and human behaviour,' he wrote in *The Human Side of Enterprise*, probably the most widely read and quoted of all the books on motivation in industry published since World War II.

The research behind Theory X and Theory Y was not original but, as McGregor acknowledged, synthesized and formulated the ideas of others (including, as Peter Drucker has observed, those Drucker himself had presented in three early books: *Concept of the Corporation, The New Society* and *The Practice of Management.*)

McGregor had already suggested the term Theory X to define a set of assumptions that had ruled management thinking since the writings of Henri Fayol. Theory X assumes that most people are lazy, dislike work and need a mixture of carrot and stick to perform; that they are basically immature, need direction and are incapable of taking responsibility. Theory Y assumes the opposite; that people actually have a psychological need to work and want achievement and responsibility – that they are adult, in fact. On this reading, Periclean Athens was a Theory Y society, Sparta a Theory X society.

McGregor believed that Theory X owed its origins to the banishment of Adam and Eve from Eden into a world where they were forced to work to survive. 'The stress that management places on productivity, on the concept of "a fair day's work," on the evils of featherbedding and restriction of output, on rewards for performance – while it has a logic in terms of the objectives of enterprise – reflects an underlying belief that management must counteract an inherent human tendency to avoid work.'

Like Maslow with his hierarchy of needs, McGregor identified a series of human wants in ascending order, from the most basic physiological urges through a desire for safety and security (and security in the workplace) to the 'social needs' such as belonging, acceptance by one's peers and the giving and receiving of affection. Above those again came the 'egoistic needs' – those that relate to an individual's self-esteem, his need for self-respect, self-confidence, autonomy, achievement, competence and knowledge; and to reputation, status, recognition and the respect of one's peers. Ultimately in McGregor's pyramid came the needs for self-fulfilment, for realizing one's individual potential and for continuing in self-development.

'Man is a wanting animal – as soon as one of his needs is satisfied, another appears in its place,' wrote McGregor in *The Human Side of Enterprise*. 'This process is unending. It continues from birth to death. Man continuously puts forth effort . . . to satisfy his needs.'

Since most modern managements by McGregor's time were providing relatively well for both physiological and safety needs, the motivational emphasis had shifted to social, egoistic and self-fulfilment needs. 'Unless there are opportunities at work to satisfy these higher-level needs, people will be deprived; and their behaviour will reflect this deprivation,' wrote McGregor.

If management continued to focus its attention on physiological needs, therefore, providing rewards was unlikely to be effective, and the only alternative under this philosophy would be reliance on the threat of punishment. Thus part of Theory X validates itself, 'but only because we have mistaken effects for causes.'

McGregor continues: 'The philosophy of management by direction and control – regardless of whether it is hard or soft – is inadequate to motivate because the human needs on which this approach relies are relatively unimportant motivators of behaviour in our society today. Direction and control are of limited value in motivating people whose important needs are social and egoistic . . . So long as the assumptions of Theory X continue to influence managerial strategy, we will fail to discover, let alone utilise, the potentialities of the average human being.'

Theory Y, the management approach designed to tap these potentialities, was based on McGregor's observations of the way management thinking had moved a considerable way from the traditional 'hard' approach and the 'soft' reaction that followed the Depression years. He formulated six basic assumptions for Theory Y:

1. 'The expenditure of physical and mental effort on work is as natural as play or rest. The average human being does not inherently dislike work. Depending upon controllable conditions, work may be a source of satisfaction

(and will be voluntarily performed) or a source of punishment (and will be avoided if possible).
2. 'External control and the threat of punishment are not the only means for bringing about effort towards organizational objectives. Man will exercise self-direction and self-control in the service of objectives to which he is committed.
3. 'Commitment to objectives is a function of the rewards associated with their achievement. The most significant of such rewards, eg the satisfaction of ego and self-actualisation needs, can be direct products of effort directed towards organizational objectives.
4. 'The average human being learns, under proper conditions, not only to accept but to seek responsibility.
5. 'The capacity to exercise a relatively high degree of imagination, ingenuity and creativity in the solution of organizational problems is widely, not narrowly, distributed in the population.
6. 'Under the conditions of modern industrial life, the intellectual potentialities of the average human being are only partially utilised.'

Such assumptions, McGregor pointed out, had a deep implication for management. Where Theory X offered management an easy scapegoat for failure – the innate nature and limitations of its human resources – Theory Y placed all problems 'squarely in the lap of management.' If employees were lazy or unwilling to show initiative or responsibility, if they were indifferent or intransigent, the fault lay in management methods. In other words, McGregor was redefining the old military adage: 'There are no bad troops, only bad officers.'

McGregor admitted that Theory Y was not perfect and remained to be tested in a variety of organizations. His disciple Abraham Maslow (qv) found it to be wanting in a well-meaning experiment run on its principles in a California electronics factory. Maslow believed it placed too much of a burden on individuals who actually wanted guidance, direction and some form of authority.

Peter Drucker has commented: 'It has now become clear

that Theory X and Theory Y are not, as McGregor maintained, theories about human nature . . . Ordinary, everyday experience teaches us that the same people react quite differently to different circumstances. They may be lazy and resist work to the point of sabotaging it in one situation. They may be motivated to achievement in another one. It is clearly not human nature nor personality structure that is at issue.'

Drucker also referred to the work of David C. McClelland of Harvard, especially his book *Motivating Economic Achievement* (Free Press, 1969), who concluded that the desire to achieve is conditioned largely by culture and experience, both of which can be changed.

McGregor never claimed that Theory Y denied all need for authority, only that it denied that authority was appropriate for all purposes, including the goal of 'obtaining commitment to objectives.'

'Theory Y assumes that people will exercise self-direction and self-control in the achievement of organizational objectives to the degree that they are committed to those objectives . . . Managerial policies and practices materially affect this degree of commitment.'

Put simply, McGregor believed that human beings were capable of far greater potential than the industrial management of his time could understand. Theory X denied even the existence of that potential: Theory Y challenged management 'to innovate, to discover new ways of organizing and directing human effort, even though we recognize that the perfect organization, like the perfect vacuum, is practically out of reach.'

(All quotations from McGregor are from *The Human Side of Enterprise*, reproduced in *Organization Theory*, ed. D. S. Pugh (Penguin 1990).

KEY BOOKS

McGregor, D. (1960) *The Human Side of Enterprise*, New

York: McGraw-Hill.
McGregor, D. (1966) *Leadership and Motivation*, MIT press.
McGregor, D. (1967) *The Professional Manager*, New York: McGraw-Hill.

20

ABRAHAM MASLOW

(1908–1970)

The 'hierarchy of needs' in motivation

New York-born psychologist and behavioural scientist whom Peter Drucker dubbed 'the father of humanist psychology.' Maslow invented the term 'hierarchy of needs' to account for the roots of human motivation.

He trained at the University of Wisconsin and broke an academic career between 1947 and 1949 to work in industry, returning to teaching at Brandeis University, Massachusetts, where he became a professor and head of department. He then spent some further time in industry, studying Douglas McGregor's Theory Y in action at a California electronics factory, where he concluded that McGregor's theory, which he had much admired, did not work in reality because it ignored the need for the structure and certainties provided by the authoritarian Theory X.

Maslow's essential optimism about the good qualities of human nature was part of its time in the climate of the postwar years, and his ideas were influential on other behavioural scientists such as Chris Argyris (qv), McGregor himself (qv), Rensis Likert (qv) and Frederick Herzberg (qv).

Maslow's 'hierarchy of needs' postulated that once an individual's basic physiological needs had been satisfied – and these included not only warmth, food and sexual fulfilment, but also a safe, structured environment – the higher needs of love, esteem and fulfilment of personal potential would be released. His greatest insight was to realize that none of these wants is absolute; as soon as one is satisfied, the fact of its satisfaction ceases to be important.

'But what Maslow did not see,' observes Drucker in his classic *Management: Tasks, Responsibilities, Practices,*

is that a want changes in the act of being satisfied. As the economic want becomes satisfied, that is, as people no longer have to subordinate every other human need and human value to getting the next meal, it becomes less and less satisfying to obtain more economic rewards. This does not mean that the economic rewards become less important. On the contrary, while the ability of the economic reward to provide a positive incentive diminishes, its capacity to create dissatisfaction, if disappointed, rapidly increases. In Herzberg's words, economic rewards cease to be 'incentives' and become 'hygiene factors.' If not properly taken care of – that is, if there is dissatisfaction with the economic rewards – they become deterrents.

This we now know to be true of every one of Maslow's wants. As a want approaches satiety, its capacity to reward, and with it its power as an incentive, diminishes fast. But its capacity to deter, to create dissatisfaction, and to act as a disincentive, rapidly increases.'

Drucker pointed out that, once a need was satisfied, ever-greater incentives were needed to maintain the same level of satisfaction, and that in the economic sphere, the danger was that additional rewards would become progressively viewed as rights or entitlements.

Maslow's experience in the California electronics company proved valuable in applying practical research to Douglas McGregor's highly theoretical proposition ('Theory Y') that most people want to work, achieve and take responsibility; in short, that most people are naturally adult, as opposed to the 'Theory X' view of humans as basically immature and in need of direction.

Maslow's discovery – in a company which believed wholeheartedly in Theory Y – was that even an organization composed of strong and mature individuals needs the security of some structure and some direction. He criticized McGregor, his mentor, for 'inhumanity' to the weak, the vulnerable and the immature, who could not take the burden of individual responsibility. Nevertheless, he remained a convinced advocate of the underlying soundness of Theory Y and his solution was that Theory X could and should be replaced by an improved version of Theory Y. This would be more demanding in many ways than the authoritarian prescription, because it required more of individuals.

By extension, as Drucker points out, this argument applies with even more force to flexible, free-form organizations, because these place a greater load on their members than do the traditional, control-and-command structures.

KEY BOOK

Maslow, A. H. (1970) *Motivation and Personality*, New York: Harper and Row.

21

ELTON W. MAYO

(1880–1949)

*Human relations in industry and respect
for individuals*

Australian-born Mayo is regarded as the founder of
industrial sociology, particularly the 'Human Relations
Movement,' based on his discoveries in the Hawthorne
Experiments of 1927–32 of what really motivates workers
to higher performance.

A graduate of Adelaide University and a medical
student in London and Edinburgh, Mayo taught mental
and moral philosophy at the University of Queensland
between 1911 and 1919. In 1923 he emigrated to the United
States, where he worked first on a three-year research
project at a Pennsylvania textile mill, prior to joining
Harvard University as associate professor of industrial
research in 1926.

Mayo spent most of his career at Harvard, ending up
as professor of industrial research in the Graduate School
of Business Administration. He was also a consultant on
industrial problems to the postwar British Labour government led by Clement Attlee.

Elton Mayo's most important finding was to identify the
roots of work satisfaction as non-economic and to connect
them more with the interest taken in a worker's perform-

ance than with financial reward. In this, he reversed the emphasis on the incentive of monetary reward which had been the conventional wisdom ever since the writings of F. W. Taylor. Workers rejected 'Taylorism,' Mayo explained, because in spite of its aids to efficiency it was basically an imposed system, not one that took account of the employees' own views.

The vital importance of management-worker communication, a key Mayo discovery, laid the foundation for the work of many later management thinkers and writers, including Peters and Waterman (*In Search of Excellence*) and the 1950s school of sociologists headed by Chris Argyris, Frederick Herzberg and Abraham Maslow.

The Hawthorne Experiments with which Mayo's name is forever linked were named after Western Electric's Hawthorne Works in Chicago. They ran from 1927 to 1932 under Mayo's leadership (and a further five years after that), and were conducted by a team of Harvard scientists and between 75 and 100 investigators working with 20,000 Western Electric employees.

The experiments arose from an earlier series of tests by Western Electric which had involved changes in working conditions and produced unexpected results in employee performance. Two teams of workers took part in these tests, in which the lighting conditions for one group only were improved. Production in that group rose dramatically – but so it did in the group for which the lighting remained unchanged.

Mayo took this further, making as many as ten changes in working conditions such as shorter hours, varied rest-breaks and a number of incentives. Mayo's research team spent a great deal of time with the work groups – each consisting of six women – discussing the changes before they were put into effect. Output increased each time a change was made. Yet when the teams were asked to return to their original working conditions, with a 48-hour week, no incentives and no rest breaks, output rose again – indeed, to the highest ever recorded at Hawthorne. Other significant results included a decline in absenteeism of 80 per cent.

The only explanation, Mayo concluded in one of his later

works, was that the employees had gained enormously in work satisfaction by the feeling that they were teams of individuals, not cogs in a machine, and by the communication between researchers and workers, leading to everyone feeling more valued and responsible for her performance and that of the group as a whole. This sense of cohesiveness and self-esteem was more important to performance than any number of improvements in the working environment.

Although Mayo did not crystallize his findings until years after the Hawthorne Experiments, a contemporary series of interviews in the Chicago works established an equally important discovery: that worker-management conflict may often be due less to the ostensible reasons for a dispute, such as tea-breaks or insufficient light, than to basic emotional attitudes. Workers were ruled by the 'logic of sentiment,' thought Mayo, whereas managers were activated by the 'logic of cost and efficiency.' Thus, without understanding and compromise, conflict was inevitable.

The ultimate importance of the Hawthorne experiments was their demonstration, in Mayo's view, that the dour Taylorist philosophy of self-interest was disproved: that workers valued spontaneous cooperation and creative relationships among those with whom they worked, and would perform accordingly. 'The desire to stand well with one's fellows, the so-called human instinct of association, easily outweighs the merely individual interest and the logic of reasoning upon which so many spurious principles of management are based,' wrote Mayo in *The Social Problems of an Industrial Civilization*.

Mayo was not, however, against scientific management, for all that he debunked Taylor's rigid application of it. 'Observation – skill – experiment and logic – these must be regarded as the three stages of advancement,' he observed in the same book. Mayo believed that his findings disproved what he called the 'rabble hypothesis' of society as 'a horde of unorganized individuals,' each of whom 'acts in a manner calculated to secure his self-preservation or self-interest.'

Two later sociological writers, D. C. Miller and W. H. Form, developed eight principal conclusions from Mayo's researches in their book *Industrial Sociology*, quoted in J. A. C. Brown's *The Social Psychology of Industry* (1954):

(1) Work is a group activity.
(2) The social world of the adult is primarily patterned about work activity.
(3) The need for recognition, security, and sense of belonging is more important in determining a worker's morale and productivity than the physical conditions under which he works.
(4) A complaint is not necessarily an objective recital of facts; it is commonly a symptom manifesting disturbance of an individual's status position.
(5) The worker is a person whose attitudes and effectiveness are conditioned by social demands from both inside and outside the work plant.
(6) Informal groups within the work plant exercise strong social controls over the work habits and attitudes of the individual worker.
(7) The change from an established to an adaptive society . . . tends continually to disrupt the social organization of a work plant and industry generally.
(8) Group collaboration does not occur by accident; it must be planned for and developed. If group collaboration is achieved, the work relations within a work plant may reach a cohesion which resists the disrupting effects of adaptive society.

Another writer on industrial psychology in the 1950s, Gordon Rattray Taylor, estimated from his observations of firms which had put similar principles into practice that by using such methods Britain could expand its national income by 50 per cent within five years without additional capital investment, and that the price of many manufactured goods could be reduced by a third. Needless to say, the experiment has never been carried out on a sufficiently wide scale to prove or disprove his theory.

Mayo's discovery of the importance of the peer group at work led him to conclude that within each formal organization existed many informal ones which could be encouraged to greater productivity by being led to do it themselves, through interest and respect on the part of their managers.

More profoundly, Mayo believed that by creating such an atmosphere of spontaneous cooperation in industry, society at large could help to combat the postwar collapse in traditional values. This, for him, remained one of the most important tasks facing a manager. The whole Human Relations movement, as engendered by Mayo's work, became concerned with discovering, through scientific research, how to harness the motivation and commitment of individuals to corporate goals.

Mayo's contribution to management thinking was seminal. It revealed the importance, in hard bottom-line terms, of human emotions, reactions and respect to the business of managing others. It also pioneered the whole concept of proper management-worker communication – again a new idea because of the respect for the individual it required between bosses and workers.

Management, Mayo demonstrated once and for all, could only succeed in leading an organization's employees if the workers, in their informal groups, accepted that leadership without reservation. In his own words, Mayo identified the importance of the Hawthorne findings as specifying, quite clearly, that the relation of working groups to management was one of the fundamental problems of large-scale industry. Organizing teamwork – developing and sustaining cooperation – had to be a major preoccupation of management. Above all, management needed to think less about what 'we' wanted to get across to 'them' than to listen to what 'they' wanted to know and would be receptive to.

'The human relations prescription, though rarely practised, remains the classic formula,' wrote Peter Drucker in 1973. It is still too rarely practised, though every management pays lip service to it.

KEY BOOKS

Mayo, E. (1933) *The Human Problems of an Industrial*

Civilisation, London: Macmillan.

Mayo, E. (1949) *The Social Problems of an Industrial Civilisation*, London: Routledge and Kegan Paul.

22

HENRY MINTZBERG

(b.1939)

How strategy is made and how managers use their time

Canadian-born professor of management at McGill University, Montreal, whose immensely influential work falls into three main categories: strategy-making; what managers actually do with their time (as opposed to what they think they do) and how their mental processes work (the 'right brain' and 'left brain' theories), and how organizations design themselves to suit their needs.

Mintzberg, originally an engineering graduate of McGill who later studied at the Sloan School of Management, Massachusetts Institute of Technology, is one of the most accessible of management writers, with an easy style and refreshingly iconoclastic approach. His reputation is rising among those who study the arts of strategic management and planning.

Mintzberg's reputation was made by *The Nature of Managerial Work*, published in 1973, and the article in *Harvard Business Review* in 1975 which brought it to a wider public (The Manager's Job: Folklore and Fact.) In researching the book, he spent a week in each of five middle- to large-sized organizations – a consulting firm, a technology company, a hospital, a consumer goods company and a school system –

observing how chief executive officers used their time, as well as reporting other studies of managers lower down the line, ranging from factory supervisors to hospital administrators.

Far from confirming any grand all-embracing role, such as Peter Drucker proposed in his analogy of the manager as orchestra conductor, Mintzberg found that a manager's time is constantly being fragmented by interruptions, but that these appeared to produce an adrenalin of their own and to convince the manager that he was achieving a great deal through responding to the pressures of the job over a great many issues, even in summary and incomplete fashion.

'Jumping from topic to topic, he (the manager) thrives on interruptions and, more often than not, disposes of items in ten minutes or less. Though he may have fifty projects going, all are delegated. He juggles them, checking each one periodically before sending it back into orbit.'

The four definitions of managerial work laid down by Henri Fayol in 1916 – planning, organization, coordination and control – have very little bearing on actual daily routine, Mintzberg discovered. Yet, as he explained in a *Harvard Business Review* article condensing the essence of his 1973 book, 'Without a proper answer, how can we teach management? How can we design planning or information systems for managers? How can we improve the practice of management at all?'

Half the activities engaged in by Mintzberg's five CEOs lasted less than nine minutes and only ten per cent exceeded one hour in duration. 'The chief executives met a steady stream of callers and mail from the moment they arrived in the morning until they left in the evening . . . A diary study of 160 British top and middle managers found that they worked for half an hour or more without interruption about once every two days.'

'The traditional literature notwithstanding, the job of managing does not breed reflective planners; the manager responds to stimuli as an individual who is conditioned by his job to prefer live to delayed action.'

The manager also spends as much time dealing with people outside as inside the company, Mintzberg found. 'He

shuns written reports, skims periodicals and merely processes his mail.' He prefers to pick up his information verbally,
at meetings and on the telephone, and indeed relies heavily
on gossip and hearsay, inside and outside the company, to
keep him up to date.

Indeed, Mintzberg concluded in a memorable finding,
'the executives I was studying – all very competent by any
standard – were fundamentally indistinguishable from their
counterparts of 100 years ago (or 1,000 years ago, for that
matter). The information they need differs, but they seek
it in the same way; by word of mouth. Their decisions
concern modern technology, but the procedures they use
are still the same as the procedures of the nineteenth-century
manager.'

'Managers seem to cherish "soft" information, especially
gossip, hearsay and speculation. Why? The reason is its
timeliness: today's gossip may be tomorrow's fact. The
manager who is not accessible for the telephone call
informing him that his biggest customer was seen golfing
with his main competitor may read about a dramatic drop
in the next quarterly report. But by then it's too late.'

Furthermore, 'managers apparently do not write down
much of what they hear. Thus the strategic data-bank of
the organization is not in the memory of its computers but
in the minds of its managers.'

Out of all this mass of material, which baldly contra-
dicted most conventional wisdom about a manager's
activities, Mintzberg identified ten principal managerial
roles, grouped into three main areas – interpersonal,
informational and decisional.

Interpersonal roles, in his definition, comprise three
functions essential to a manager: those of figurehead,
leader, and liaison. The first two are self-explanatory (the
figurehead performs ceremonial roles such as making
presentation speeches, meeting visiting dignitaries and
lunching important clients; the leader hires, trains and
motivates employees) while the third covers a manager's
network of relationships within and without the organization, outside his vertical chain of command, and mainly in
pursuit of building up a private information system.

'Managers spend as much time with peers and other people outside their units as they do with their own subordinates, and surprisingly little time with their own superiors.'

Informational roles involve those of monitor (keeping tabs on what's going on); disseminator (transmitting essential information to subordinates) and spokesman (the public voice of the unit). 'The manager emerges as the nerve centre of his organizational unit. He may not know everything, but he typically knows more than any member of his staff . . . Many of these contacts are with other managers of equal status, who are themselves nerve centres in their own organization. In this way the manager develops a powerful data base of information. The processing of information is a key part of the manager's job . . . In large part, communication is his work.'

Decisional roles, not surprisingly, are described as the most important. Mintzberg divides this category into four – entrepreneur, disturbance handler, resource allocator and negotiator.

As entrepreneur, the manager 'seeks to improve his unit and to adapt it to changing conditions' sometimes juggling as many as fifty different projects at a time, such as initiating a PR campaign, dealing with a poor cash-flow position, reorganizing a weak department or looking after the various stages of an acquisition. As disturbance handler, the manager reacts to events and change beyond his foresight or control; a strike, the bankruptcy of a major customer or the failure of a key supplier.

It is here that Mintzberg parts company most strikingly with Drucker's comparison of the manager's role to that of an orchestral conductor. 'In effect, every manager must spend a good part of his time responding to high-pressure disturbances.'

As resource allocator, the manager must decide how best to deploy the assets of the organization, including its human assets and, most importantly, the manager's own time. As negotiator, he is responsible for all the variety of decisions involved in dealing with other individuals; whether these concern a difficult sales contract, the threat of a strike, staff grievances or attracting a new star player to the team.

All the variables contained within these permutations led Mintzberg to conclude that management is an art rather than a teachable science, and that it requires a continuous process of self-education and assessment. He also pointed out that the roles are part of an integrated whole and cannot easily be separated when, for example, efforts are made to split a managerial job into internal and external roles, though not all managers, he found, give equal attention to all roles. (Sales managers tend to emphasize the interpersonal side, production managers the decisional roles and staff managers the informational roles.)

In summarizing the theme of his findings for the *Harvard Business Review* in 1975, Mintzberg said the pressures of his job 'drive the manager to be superficial in his actions – to overload himself with work, encourage interruption, respond quickly to every stimulus, seek the tangible and avoid the abstract, make decisions in small increments and do everything abruptly . . . the danger in managerial work is that (managers) will respond to every issue equally (and that means abruptly) and that they will never work the tangible bits and pieces of informational input into a comprehensive picture of their work.'

Management schools, he concluded, would only begin 'the serious training of managers when skill training takes a serious place next to cognitive learning. . . . Cognitive learning no more makes a manager than it does a swimmer. The latter will drown the first time he jumps into the water if his coach never takes him out of the lecture hall, gets him wet and gives him feedback on his performance.'

Managerial skills such as developing peer relationships, resolving conflicts, handling information and negotiations need to be practised, and the manager should be introspective enough about his work to go on learning on the job.

'No job is more vital to our society than that of the manager,' declared Mintzberg. 'It is the manager who determines whether our institutions serve us well or whether they squander our talents and resources. It is time to strip away the folklore about managerial work, and time to study it realistically so that we can begin the difficult task of making significant improvements in its performance.'

From analysing the components of managerial work, Mintzberg moved on to study the design of organizations in *The Structuring of Organizations* (1979) and *Structures in Fives: Designing Effective Organizations* (1983).

He concluded that most organizational structures fall into five basic categories: simple structure, machine bureaucracy, professional bureaucracy, divisionalized form and adhocracy – a term recently appropriated and redefined by Robert Waterman to describe the ideal conditions for a flexible, innovation-inducing organizational structure. (Waterman, author of *The Renewal Factor* and co-author with Tom Peters of the massively selling *In Search of Excellence*, acknowledges Mintzberg as one of his own most influential gurus.)

Mintzberg's simple structure organization is just that: a centralized, perhaps autocratic arrangement typical of the entrepreneur-founded company. There will be only a small hierarchy, and control is exercised by a strong chief executive. It is the sort of organization that attracts strong loyalty because of its simplicity, flexibility, informality and 'sense of mission' – but it is desperately vulnerable to the accidents of fate: 'one heart attack can literally wipe out the organization's prime co-ordinating mechanism.'

The machine bureaucracy, by contrast, gains its strength from what Mintzberg calls its 'technostructure' – its financial controllers, strategic planners, production experts. It is best at mass-production tasks and is characterized by many layers of management and formal procedures. It tends to be slow on its feet when reacting to change, and poor at motivating its employees. A large car assembly plant would be a typical example.

The professional bureaucracy is built less on hierarchy than on shared expertise – it might be a professional practice of some kind, a school or a hospital. Its administration is governed by standards set by independent professional bodies. It will tend to be more democratic and more highly motivated – among the professionals, if not their support workers – than the machine bureaucracy, but with its lines of authority less clearly set out.

The divisionalized form is reflected in the typical large

multinational or industrial corporation where a small central core controls key guidelines for a number of otherwise autonomous units. Essentially, Mintzberg sees this as an offshoot of the machine bureaucracy – several machine bureaucracies, in fact, operating under a central staff. It may have started life as a single machine bureaucracy which hived off into divisions as a result of geographic market diversifications.

The adhocracy is most often found in the new technology industries, which need constantly to innovate and respond quickly to changing markets. It is characterized by flexible, cross-border teams collaborating on specific projects as required, and of Mintzberg's five categories of organization 'shows the least reverence for the classical principles of management.'

Mintzberg's adhocracy has two sub-sections; the operating adhocracy, a creative unit working in the competitive marketplace, such as an advertising agency or software development company, and the administrative adhocracy, which may be research-based, like NASA.

Within Mintzberg's five basic organizational structures are five common elements: the 'strategic apex' of top executives (strongest in the simple structure); the 'techno-structure' of key individuals in finance, training, personnel, planning and production (strongest in the machine bureaucracy); the 'operating core' of those at the coalface of the organization (nurses and teachers in a professional bureaucracy, buyers and sales staff in a manufacturing machine bureaucracy); the 'middle line' of managers who link the strategic apex with the operating core (strongest in the divisionalized form); and finally, the 'support staff', who work in areas such as R&D, salaries, public relations and so on. In a manufacturing company their role, though important, is not the fulcrum that it is in the adhocracy, which relies on the quality of its R&D.

'If Simple Structure and Machine Bureaucracy were yesterday's structures, and Professional Bureaucracy and the Divisionalised Form are today's, then Adhocracy is clearly tomorrow's,' writes Mintzberg. But he does not rule out further evolutions of structure as different influences exert their pull, and he has identified one for the future, where ideological influences are involved, which he calls the Missionary. Examples include the Israeli kibbutz and the Japanese manufacturing company.

In 1989 Mintzberg distilled 20 years of his thinking into *Mintzberg on Management*, the best introduction to his work, which also includes a chapter on 'crafting strategy' – how this important managerial function works – and the concept that helped shape his understanding of the process, the different part played by the right and left hemispheres of the brain in managerial work.

Briefly, Mintzberg has established a theory that successful chief executives favour the right-hand or intuitive side of their brain more than the left-hand or analytical side. Creative strategy, he argues, requires 'right brain' thinking and there is more than logical planning to the effective management of an organization. 'Effective managers seem to revel in ambiguity, in complex, mysterious systems with relatively little order.'

He supports his theory with some general observations of managers at work, while emphasizing that, as a theory, it still remains largely in the realm of speculation.

Nevertheless, he is convinced that 'the important policy-level processes required to manage an organization rely to a considerable extent on the faculties identified with the brain's right hemisphere.'

And in typically iconoclastic style, he adds that if his suggestions turn out to be valid, teachers of management had better 'revise drastically some of their notions about management education. Unfortunately, the revolution in that sphere over the last 15 years – while it has brought so much of value – has virtually consecrated the modern management school to the worship of the left hemisphere . . . There is a need for a new balance in our schools, the balance that the best of human brains can achieve, between the analytic and the intuitive.'

KEY BOOKS

Mintzberg, H. (1973, 1980) *The Nature of Managerial Work*, New York: Harper and Row.

Mintzberg, H. (1979) *The Structuring of Organizations*, New Jersey: Prentice-Hall.

Mintzberg, H. (1983) *Structures in Fives: Designing Effective Organizations*, New Jersey: Prentice-Hall.

Mintzberg, H. (1983) *Power in and Around Organizations*, New Jersey: Prentice-Hall.

Mintzberg, H. (1989) *Mintzberg on Management*, New York: The Free Press; London: Collier Macmillan.

23

KENICHI OHMAE

(b.1943)

Lessons from Japanese global business strategy

Japan's only world-class management guru, Kenichi Ohmae is the head of McKinsey's Tokyo office and a leading international exponent of global business strategy.

Ohmae, who trained as a nuclear physicist at MIT, has published around 30 books and articles on strategy and is renowned for the insights he offers into Japanese strategic thinking and its relationship to Japan's competitive strength in world markets.

In Ohmae's view, western management thinkers have rarely succeeded in analysing Japanese strategic management styles, focusing instead on tactics like quality circles and company songs. There is a failure, Ohmae considers, to recognize the most fundamental difference between eastern and western strategy – that Japanese companies plan for the long term, western ones for short-term profits.

Ohmae's two most influential books are *The Mind of the Strategist*, first published in 1982, and *Triad Power* (1985), in which he argued that companies which fail to establish themselves inside all three major trading blocs – Europe, the US and the Pacific Rim – become fatally vulnerable to competition from those which do so. The 'three Cs' – commitment, competitiveness and creativity – form his prescription for success in the Triad. *The Mind of the Strategist*, subtitled in its first edition The Art of

Japanese Business, is a highly readable exploration of techniques that can be developed to match the mixture of analysis and intuition which many Japanese business leaders bring to their strategic planning.

Following the publication of *In Search of Excellence* by two of his US McKinsey colleagues, Tom Peters and Robert Waterman, Ohmae embarked on his own study of excellent companies for the Japanese market.

A colleague of Ohmae's at McKinsey summed up his approach as: 'He questions everything. He's always asking "Why?"'. His latest work, *The Borderless World*, reinforced his gadfly reputation with its bold contentions, among them his view that the trade imbalance between the US and Japan is an 'illusion created by accounting systems that are tragically out of date.'

Of all the scores of books produced by management gurus since World War II, Kenichi Ohmae's *The Mind of the Strategist* has a good claim to be the most practical teaching aid to the development of higher management skills. His objective was to show how outstanding strategists – who in Japan often lack a formal business education – go about developing the ideas that solve problems and create opportunities for their companies. It is less a formula than a set of concepts and approaches which can help anyone to develop this valuable mental agility.

What business strategy is all about, says Ohmae, 'what distinguishes it from all other kinds of business planning, is . . . competitive advantage.' Corporate strategy, he argues, implies an attempt 'to alter a company's strength relative to that of its competitors in the most efficient way.'

Intuition and insight, in Ohmae's view, are more effective keys to successful strategy than rational analysis, though this has its place in the process. 'In what I call the mind of the strategist, insight and a consequent drive for achievement, often amounting to a sense of mission, fuel a thought process which is basically creative and intuitive rather than rational,' he writes.

He defines creative insight as 'the ability to combine, synthesise or reshuffle previously unrelated phenomena in such a way that you get more out of the emergent whole than you have put in.' If creativity cannot be taught, he maintains, it can certainly be consciously cultivated. How it can be cultivated in people with no natural talent for strategy, or in a corporate culture at odds with creative thinking, forms the core of Ohmae's book.

An earlier book, *The Corporate Strategist* (1975) attempted to do it in a specifically Japanese context. *The Mind of the Strategist* is larded with Japanese case studies – how Honda, Toyota or Matsushita, for instance, created new markets or challenged successful competitors – but its application is universal.

The book is organized under three main headings: 'The Art of Strategic Thinking,' 'Building Successful Strategies', and 'Modern Strategic Realities.' The first explores the basic mental processes involved – dissecting a problem or situation into its constituent parts; asking the right 'solution-oriented' questions, constructing 'issue diagrams' and 'profit diagrams' to facilitate getting to the right diagnosis.

Ohmae identifies the 'four routes to strategic advantage' – strategy based on a company's key factors for success in its capability to increase market share and profitability; strategy based on exploiting any relative superiority; strategy based on aggressive initiatives, challenging accepted assumptions; and strategy based on 'strategic degrees of freedom' (SDF) – development of innovations such as new markets or products.

All four options are examined in depth with case studies drawn from Japanese industry. As an example of aggressive initiative, he cites Toyota's Taiichi Ohno questioning the need to stockpile large quantities of components for the production line. Ohno's question eventually led to the introduction of 'Just-in-Time,' and a revolution in production systems worldwide.

'If, instead of accepting the first answer, one . . . persists in asking "Why?" four or five times in succession, one will certainly get to the guts of the issue, where fundamental bottlenecks and problems lie.'

Strategic degrees of freedom also require the recognition of changes in the users' (customers') objective function (such as a preference for compact physical size in stereo equipment over performance measured by power output – part of Sony's rise in the market – or the perception by Honda and other car companies that many customers were switching from speed and prestige to convenience, economy and utility.)

'Stretching one's mind to find the SDF by which the new objectives can be satisfied is one way to become a pioneer in the new-business game,' Ohmae observes.

Ohmae advises trainee strategists not to worry overmuch about details that seem to threaten their plans. Write down each point of uncertainty, he counsels, and assess its positive or negative outcome. If the overall result won't be affected by a few negative factors, follow the example of Japanese entrepreneurs such as Konosuke Matsushita and Soichiro Honda and persist with execution of the plan.

Responsiveness to changing customer objectives lies at the root of Ohmae's system for constructing a business strategy. His three points of the 'strategic triangle' are the corporation (its strengths, weaknesses and resources), the customer and the competition.

'Customer-based strategies are the basis of all strategy,' asserts Ohmae. He is convinced that a corporation's foremost concern should be the interest of its customers as opposed to that of its shareholders or other parties. 'In the long run the corporation that is genuinely interested in its customers is the one that will be interesting to investors.'

Ohmae's book goes on to analyse competitive advantage by price, volume and cost and their effect on profitability. 'If, for example, you can get a better price because of better design, you may be able to achieve better profit performance than your competitors.'

Having set out strategic mechanisms for single businesses, Ohmae then integrates them into a corporate structure, looking at such techniques as Product Portfolio Management (PPM), a corporate idea for large, diverse businesses, based on the principles of managing an investment portfolio.

In the 'Strategic Realities' section, Ohmae sets his planning process against five 'key economic trends' which he believes will have an important impact on business strategies in the coming decade. In 1982, these were:

1. Continuing low growth.
2. Market maturity and strategic stalemate.
3. Uneven distribution of resources (eg Opec oil).
4. Growing international complexities.
5. Irreversible inflation.

Ohmae lists seven major changes likely to influence business strategies in the 1990s:

1. A shift from labour-intensive to capital-intensive industries.
2. A shift from multinational to 'multi-local' companies.
3. A shift in the fixed to variable cost ratio.
4. A shift from steel to electronics-based industries.
5. A shift in business unit definition.
6. A shift from international to local financial management.
7. A shift to a coordinated corporate value system.

Ohmae's iconoclastic books on global business strategy have made him an international celebrity on the lecture circuit. He says that he is now more interested in 'society, social systems and large corporate activities on a global scale . . . Interdependence is the key to making our world work.'

The Borderless World (1990) has an important message for large companies in the 1990s. 'Too few managers,' says Ohmae, 'consciously try to set plans and build organisations as if they see all key customers equidistant from the corporate centre . . . The word "overseas" has no place in Honda's vocabulary because it sees itself as equidistant from all key customers.'

KEY BOOKS

Ohmae, K. (1982, 1983) *The Mind of the Strategist*, New York: McGraw-Hill; London: Penguin Business Library.

Ohmae, K. (1985) *Triad Power: the Coming Shape of Global Competition*, New York: Free Press.

Ohmae, K. (1990) *The Borderless World*, New York: Harper Business; London: Collins.

24

RICHARD T. PASCALE

(b.1938)

The creative use of conflict in organizations

Former consultant to McKinsey who collaborated with Peters and Waterman, of *In Search of Excellence*, in developing the 'Seven-S' system of measuring a company for excellence. The 'hard' S factors were strategy, structure and systems; the 'soft' S factors – at which Japanese companies excelled – were style, shared values (or superordinate goals), skills and staff.

The Art of Japanese Management, which Pascale co-authored with Anthony Athos in 1981, used the system to illuminate brilliantly the differences in management culture between Japan and the US, encapsulated in close-up studies of Matsushita Electric and ITT and their respective chief executives.

A Stanford University professor and leading management consultant, Pascale moved in the late 1980s to a new perspective on management priorities in a world where nothing could be safely predicted except chaos and discontinuity.

Managing On the Edge (1990) examined how underlying paradigms or habits of thought in organizations filter and subtly distort a full understanding of change. A central theme of the book, which was hailed by the *Financial Times* as more intellectually stimulating than *In Search of Excellence*, is that the ultimate, and largely ignored, task of management is one of creating and breaking paradigms, and that success in organizations breeds failure unless there is a system in place that constantly encourages debate, even contention and conflict, leading to a process of continued renewal.

The Art of Japanese Management hit its moment precisely, as did *In Search of Excellence* a year later. US business leaders were increasingly worried about the growing power of Japanese companies and the competitive edge they were gaining in Western markets. The book that could crack the Japanese secret for them was bound to become a best-seller.

Pascale and Athos not only identified the reasons for Japanese competitive excellence but what enabled organizations in Japan to continue performing to superior standards over time. The answer was the Seven S model, and how the best Japanese enterprises used the Western managerial 'hard S' levers to a more productive purpose by allying them with the 'soft S' levers.

In one of the most gripping narratives to be found in management literature, Pascale and Athos held a mirror up in turn to leading exemplars of the two business cultures – Matsushita Electric, run by its founder Konosuke Matsushita, and ITT, then managed by the formidable hard man of American business, Harold Geneen.

Like Peters and Waterman after them, Pascale and Athos found that many of the best-performing US companies that had sustained their vitality over time were just as efficient as the Japanese at synchronizing hard and soft S values. 'The best firms link their purposes and ways of realising them to human values as well as to economic measures like profit and efficiency,' they observed.

Remarking that many observers of the Japanese phenomenon tended to view it through American cultural filters and therefore assumed the soft S factors to be mere froth, the authors produced a memorable image: 'That "froth" has the power of the Pacific.'

Along with its two close-up case studies, the book

analyses each of the Seven S levers of management and uses a musical analogy to express how they work as a whole; particularly how the bass clef in music, which carries the rhythms under the treble clef melody (rhythms which hold much of the power of music over the listener) equates to the deeper meanings conveyed to a company's workforce about its management's real values.

For this reason, 'superordinate goals', which Pascale later rechristened 'shared values', are the hidden key to the power of the soft S factors. 'Superordinate goals provide the glue that holds the other six together.'

These goals are analysed under six headings:

- The company as an entity
- The company's external markets
- The company's internal operations
- The company's employees
- The company's relation to society and the state
- The company's relation to culture, including religion

(This section of the book maps out the groundwork for much subsequent writing on corporate culture.)

In their study of the two multinationals, Matsushita and ITT, Pascale and Athos drew comparisons in such areas as marketing, financial methods, research, strategic planning policies and – the key factor – in the styles of management practised by Konosuke Matsushita and Harold Geneen.

The authors found the US company generally comparable with the Japanese one as far as hard S factors were concerned. The crucial difference lay in the soft S areas: in consequence, they suggested, US companies tend to be wasteful of human resources while the Japanese, as is natural to their culture of interdependence and consensus, have a far more productive and collaborative boss/subordinate relationship.

The originality of the book lay in its cultural approach to management and its holistic approach. One of its biggest contributions, Pascale feels, was to introduce the concept of shared values, that companies need to consider the values they stand for and to be concerned with 'meaning as well as money.' It continues to be essential reading.

Pascale's first major 'solo' book, *Managing On the Edge*, is likely to prove just as important to management thinking in its time. Like Peters' *Thriving On Chaos*, it addresses the need for a radical reappraisal of conventional management wisdom, especially in the area of managing change and disruption in the business environment.

Although Pascale had worked with Peters and Waterman on the preparation for *In Search of Excellence*, he came to feel that *Excellence* and other books like it were shallow and had resulted in a series of management fads that failed to address the needs of managements wanting to develop and maintain excellence within their organizations.

Managing On the Edge, subtitled 'How the smartest companies use conflict to stay ahead,' takes the decline of successful corporations as its point of departure and examines how underlying paradigms or mind-sets blind managements to the first weak signals of change. A central premise of the book is that the ultimate, and largely ignored, task of management is one of creating and breaking paradigms. Constructive use of contention, Pascale argues, coupled with persistent self-questioning, is the most common quality to be found in the world's best self-sustaining firms.

Pascale's thesis is that success breeds failure unless there is a system that constantly encourages debate and thus leads to a process of continued organizational renewal. Even excellent organizations can persist with perceptions formed in the period of their greatest success and never questioned since. Their great strengths become the roots of weakness because they resist change and are unable to see environmental change happening around them.

The book identifies a process of questioning and renewal that is part organizational and part attitude. In order to be creative and to adapt to changing circumstances, the organization needs to have controlled conflict and questioning. The book explains this concept and gives case examples, featuring some of America's leading multinational companies (Ford alone gets 60 pages), of how organizations can foster the creative tensions necessary for renewal.

Pascale explores how certain pioneering Western and Japanese companies – he rates Honda one of the best managed companies in the world – become 'engines of inquiry,' mechanisms for continuous learning and renewal. They do it by building on the 'Seven S' levers of management – strategy, structure, systems, style, staff, shared values and skills – each of which involves a paradoxical tradeoff. Stimulating and managing the creative tension of these tradeoffs maintains the necessary restlessness and vitality for corporate renewal.

Pascale advocates an active 'orchestration of tension' and cites Honda's (and now Ford's) ceaseless preoccupation with examining and assessing what it does and how it does it. The most successful corporate leaders, Pascale concludes, constantly challenge their own assumptions and limitations, and seek new and enlarged paradigms.

Change, he points out, 'did not find its way into Honda, Ford and General Electric through quick fixes. It happened when each company's leadership adopted new ways of thinking . . . . With discontinuous change, leadership leaps into the unknown.'

Honda, he believes, has developed mechanisms to channel the forces of constructive contention in a way that keeps the company 'in a sort of restless, uneasy state, which enables it to get a great deal out of its people and itself as an entity.' But if the company were to get too comfortable with itself and become set in its successful patterns, then it too would decline along with other 'excellent' companies.

Citicorp is cited as an example of a company that's 'living dangerously' by maintaining a 'Darwinian' culture in which jobs are always at risk and judged by each day's peformance. Under Walter Wriston, who changed Citicorp's perception of its business as one of moving information rather than one of moving money, the company harnessed tension to make an aggressive impact in a staid industry. But such a level of tension, creating a lot of personal insecurity, could turn against itself if the balance were lost.

The same failure of success can occur if a company such as Hewlett-Packard takes its mission of vision and values to such lengths that they become a behavioural straitjacket. 'So if there is one prescription,' Pascale has commented, 'it is that there is no prescription. Or that any prescription taken to extremes is going to cause trouble.'

Pascale believes that in the next 60 years the Western world will see a 'significant enlargement' of the fundamentals of good management. 'What I want to do is to enlist every thoughtful person into an inquiry about what really makes organizations tick, because I think that the task of thinking more deeply is going to serve us all well, not shovelling still another solution onto the plate of managers who have had too many "solutions" already.'

KEY BOOKS

Pascale, R. T. and Athos, A. G. (1981, 1982, 1986) *The Art of Japanese Management*, New York: Simon and Schuster; London: Allen Lane; Penguin Books
Pascale, R. T. (1990) *Managing On the Edge*, New York: Simon and Schuster; London: Viking.

25

TOM PETERS AND ROBERT H. WATERMAN JR

(b.1942) (b.1936)

The 'excellence' cult and prescriptions for managing chaotic change

Tom Peters and Robert Waterman will forever be linked because of the phenomenal success of *In Search of Excellence*, although it was the only book the two former McKinsey consultants wrote together. Since its publication in 1982, each has carved out his own distinctive niche in authorship and on the lecture trail.

Excellence is by far the world's best-selling business book. It was slow to take off on both sides of the Atlantic, but its reputation rocketed by word of mouth and suddenly companies were ordering '50, 100, 200 copies to give to their executives,' as the British publisher recalls. It reached the million mark in sales in record time, within a year, and has now sold over 5m copies. Despite the fact that two-thirds of its 'excellent' companies have since faded in performance – Peters began his 1987 book *Thriving On Chaos* with the bold words, 'There are no excellent companies' – *In Search of Excellence* still endlessly reprints in paperback and its distinctive black, white and gold cover continues to walk off the airport bookstalls where most business books are sold in the UK.

Before joining McKinsey in 1974, Peters worked in the Pentagon for two years, where he became 'fascinated by complex organisations.' He then took a master's degree in civil engineering at Cornell University before serving in Vietnam. Later, he took an MBA at Stanford and worked again in Washington for the Office of Management and Budget. Today, he and Michael Porter can probably claim to be the most sought-after and expensive management lecturers in the world. The Tom Peters Group has built a huge business in videos, cassettes and TV series as well as personal appearances and consultancy work.

Bob Waterman is the complete temperamental opposite of the excitable, hyper-active Peters, whose shirts are rapidly soaked with sweat as he delivers his quickfire, floor-pacing lectures. A tall, laid-back Californian, Waterman says he could, if he chose, do as many lectures as Peters – roughly one every other day – but he observes laconically: 'Why kill myself?' Running his own consultancy in San Francisco for two days a week, giving 24 to 30 lectures a year and advising several smallish companies in a board capacity suits him better than Peters' hectic travelling schedule.

Waterman spent twenty-one years with McKinsey, initially working on the restructuring and decentralization of large organizations. He worked in Japan and Australia and in 1976 returned to San Francisco, where the partnership with Peters began. Both men left the firm after *Excellence* was published – Peters first, then Waterman in 1986 – and although they considered another co-authorship, McKinsey was not enthusiastic once Peters had left, so Peters wrote the sequel, *A Passion for Excellence*, with Nancy Austin.

Peters' work took a new direction with *Thriving on Chaos* (1987), which inaugurated a genre of books on managing change. Waterman's *The Renewal Factor*, also published in 1987, developed some of the ideas in *Excellence*, chiefly the principle of learning from the best, but it also focused on the need for managers to ride and manage change and unpredictability.

Waterman's own favourite management reading includes what he calls the 'heavy-duty' theoretical works of Karl Weick on organizations, Alfred Chandler's *Strategy and Structure*, the work of Chester Barnard, Elton Mayo's Hawthorne experiments ('they showed that just paying attention to things gets more done'), Drucker's *Managing for Results*, Mintzberg on how managers spend their time, and Warren Bennis, especially his earlier works on organization development ('a little like Drucker but more theoretical'). Recently, the book that has most influenced him is James Gleick's *Chaos*, a brilliant *tour de force* on the unpredictable nature of life. 'It's important stuff, an entirely new branch of mathematics. It's as if calculus were re-invented. It has a lot to say about the inherent unforecastability of things, and why things we put a lot of faith in don't work. It has a lot to say about stock markets.'

Waterman believes that F. W. Taylor's work has been 'something of a touchstone' and that we are 'still living in a world created by Taylor; the specialisation of work, mechanising things, dividing work up into functions.' However much they would deny it, he suggests, many managers still essentially practise Taylorism.

In his latest book *Adhocracy: the Power to Change*, Waterman has developed a concept pioneered by Drucker and Mintzberg (and Alvin Toffler in *Future Shock*), concerning innovative project teams operating across a company's departmental boundaries. He is currently working on an aspect of companies that would not have been fully understood before the 1990s, identifying how businesses establish themselves favourably in the public consciousness; 'the things that make people feel good about a company.' These include, says Waterman, total quality, self-directed teams, business and social responsibility . . . . businesses that are doing well yet behaving responsibly, 'that are going beyond the idea of just making a buck.'

Peters and Waterman have almost branded the word 'excellence' as a branch of management theory. Their phenomenally successful book has spawned a host of imitators and was the subject of a fascinated study by Japan's Kenichi Ohmae, also a McKinsey man. At the time, though, Waterman says they had no idea it would prove such a watershed.

Its simple idea was the extension of a McKinsey project begun in 1977, to analyse the lessons from 43 of *Fortune's* top 500 companies that had consistently beaten their competitors over twenty years by six financial yardsticks:

- Compound asset growth
- Compound equity growth
- Ratio of market value to book value
- Return on capital
- Return on equity
- Return on sales

Peters and Waterman developed the famous McKinsey 'Seven-S' formula to analyse an organization: structure, strategy, systems, style of management, skills (corporate strengths), staff and shared values. Applying this framework to their 43 companies, they identified their eight by now well-known characteristics shared by all of them:

- A bias for action: getting on with it
- Close to the customer: learning from the people they serve
- Autonomy and entrepreneurship: fostering innovation and nurturing 'champions'
- Productivity through people; treating the rank and file as a source of quality
- Hands-on, value-driven: management showing its commitment
- Stick to the knitting: stay with the business you know
- Simple form, lean staff: some of the best companies have a minimum of headquarters staff
- Simultaneous loose-tight properties; autonomy in shop floor activities plus centralized values

All their 43 companies, Peters and Waterman found, were 'brilliant on the basics.' Also, in almost every case, a strong leader had been influential at some stage in forming the culture of excellence.

Five years after the book's publication, two-thirds of those companies had hit trouble in varying degrees, among them Atari, Avon, Wang and DuPont. Only 14 could still be classified as excellent by the original criteria.

Peters and Waterman individually concluded that nothing in today's chaotic business environment stays the same long enough for excellence of the sustained type possible before 1982 to be developed. In *Thriving on Chaos* he cited IBM – 'declared dead in 1979, the best of the best in 1982, and dead again in 1986.' People Express, one star of their book, collapsed completely.

Excellence, suggested P&W, required re-defining – excellent firms were now those that believed only in constant improvement and the demands of constant change.

A key concept behind *Thriving on Chaos*, a title that struck a chord with many gurus in the late 80s, was the need to move from a hierarchical management pyramid to a horizontal, fast, cross-functional, cooperative one.

Peters evolved 45 precepts for managers of every level. They ran as follows:

- Quality revolution
- Become a service addict
- Achieve total customer responsiveness
- Become true internationalists, both small and large firms
- Strive to achieve uniqueness
- Listen to customers, end users, suppliers, retailers
- Make manufacturing the prime marketing tool
- 'Over-invest' in people, frontline sales, service, distribution (make these the company heroes)
- Become customer-obsessed
- Develop an innovation strategy
- Use multi-function teams for all development activities
- Substitute pilots and prototypes for proposals
- Ignore 'Not Invented Here' and learn to adapt from the best (practise 'creative swiping')
- Use systematic word of mouth for launching
- Applaud champions
- Symbolize innovativeness
- Support failures by publicly rewarding well thought-out

mistakes
- Measure innovation
- Make innovation a way of life for everyone
- Involve all personnel in all functions in virtually everything
- Organize as much as possible around teams
- Invest time in recruiting
- Invest in human capital as much as hardware
- Provide bold financial incentives for all
- Guarantee continuous employment for a large slice of the workforce
- Radically reduce layers of management
- Re-conceive middle managers as facilitators instead of guardians
- Reduce and simplify paperwork and bureaucratic procedures
- Challenge conventional management wisdom on a day-to-day basis
- Develop and live an 'enabling and empowering vision' (effective leadership at all levels is marked by a core philosophy [values] and a vision of how the enterprise or department wishes to make its mark)
- Lead by personal example
- Practise visible management
- Become a compulsive listener
- Ensure that frontline people know they are the heroes
- Examine each act of delegation and increase it radically
- Destroy bureaucratic baggage
- Focus on exactly what you have changed recently – what your subordinates have changed. Ask the question a dozen times a day at least, induce a sense of urgency throughout
- Develop simple systems to encourage participation and understanding
- Simplify control systems (eg performance appraisals, setting of objectives, job descriptions)
- Share information with everyone
- Set conservative financial targets
- Demand total integrity in all dealings, both inside and outside the firm

Waterman's prescriptions for renewing vitality and performance in *The Renewal Factor* numbered just eight:

- Informed opportunism: 'The renewing companies treat
  information as their main strategic advantage, and
  flexibility as their main strategic weapon.'
- Direction and empowerment: 'The renewing companies
  treat everyone as a source of creative input . . . Their
  managers define the boundaries and their people figure
  out the best way of doing the job within these
  boundaries.'
- Friendly facts, congenial controls: 'The renewing companies treat facts as friends and financial controls as
  liberating.'
- A different mirror: ability to step outside the company
  and look at it from a different perspective
- Teamwork, trust, politics and power: the first two are
  common to all renewing companies, the last two never
  found.
- Causes and commitment: 'Commitment results from
  management's ability to turn grand causes into small
  actions so everyone can contribute.'
- Attitudes and attention: 'Visible management attention,
  rather than exhortation, gets things done.'
- Stability in motion: renewing companies have a 'habit of
  habit-breaking'.

Peters and Waterman together were responsible for popular-
izing the study of management to a mass readership, and
initiating a new direction in management thinking. No other
authors have come near their feat with *Excellence* in the
number of copies sold. They illuminated many issues, such
as corporate culture and values, which are just as valid today
as in 1982. As the business environment changed and became
subject to more shocks and discontinuities, they responded
with their individual views of managing change – a concept
that few companies understood a decade ago, but which is
now central to industrial survival.

KEY BOOKS

Peters, T. and Waterman, R. H. Jr. (1982) *In Search of Excellence*, New York and London: Harper and Row.
Peters, T. and Austin, N. (1985) *A Passion for Excellence*, London: Collins.
Peters, T. (1987) (1988) *Thriving on Chaos*, New York: Alfred A. Knopf; London: Macmillan.
Waterman, R. H. Jr. (1987) *The Renewal Factor*, New York: Bantam.

26

MICHAEL PORTER

(b.1947)

*Strategies for competitive advantage, both
national and international*

Harvard Business School's star professor (of general
management) and regarded by many leading US businessmen as the world's greatest expert on strategies for
competitive advantage. With stratospheric lecture fees
and four books on competitive strategy that have earned
him over $2m in royalties, Porter is the most fashionable
and sought-after of the younger gurus on the international circuit, rivalled only by Tom Peters, co-founder of the
'excellence' cult.

In the summer of 1990, *Business Week* described
Porter as 'a business phenomenon in his own right' and
'one of the highest paid academics anywhere.' He is
booked for lectures six months in advance and has sold
over $3m worth of video seminars. The consultancy he
co-founded occupies him four days a month, advising
big-name companies. Porter himself acknowledges that
he has become a 'brand' for which buyers are willing to
pay.

Porter joined the Harvard faculty at the age of twenty-
six after earning an economics doctorate there. Earlier, at
Princeton, he had graduated in aeronautical engineering
and reached professional standard at golf. His first book,
Competitive Strategy (1980), has sold over 300,000 copies
and is deemed by many on both sides of the Atlantic to
be the definitive work on corporate strategy. His latest,

The Competitive Advantage of Nations, analyses the reasons for ten countries' ability to gain global market share in certain industries. (The UK comes out with a depressingly peripheral list, aside from chemicals and pharmaceuticals: Porter deems it a world leader, for example, in auctioneering and biscuit manufacture. Britain scores only seven world-challenging categories to Switzerland's 16 and Denmark's 11.) The substantial tome, a surprise best-seller on airport bookstalls, is spinning off four 'sons', each based on an individual country – a good example of Porter's own flair for competitive advantage.

The very words 'competitive strategy' or 'competitive advantage' are enough to identify Michael Porter wherever management gurus gather. Some critics claim that his ideas for analysing markets and industries are based on old economic theories, and Porter himself has acknowledged his debt to Joseph A. Schumpeter, among others, in *The Competitive Advantage of Nations.* What he does brilliantly, however, is to package and simplify analytical models that would otherwise be dauntingly difficult for most working businessmen to understand. His seminars, in particular, are as lively as those of Tom Peters.

On joining the Harvard faculty, Porter was among the first to project corporate strategy in marketplace terms rather than as a theoretical concept linking various functions in an organization.

His basic tool for managers seeking to analyse their own company's competitive position employs five factors or forces that drive competition;

- Existing rivalry between firms
- The threat of new entrants to a market
- The threat of substitute products and services
- The bargaining power of suppliers
- The bargaining power of buyers

134

He then identifies five generic descriptions of industries: fragmented, emerging, mature, declining and global.

Porter says a firm may possess two kinds of competitive advantage: low cost or differentiation. 'Competitive advantage is a function of either providing comparable buyer value more efficiently than competitors (low cost), or performing activities at comparable cost but in unique ways that create more buyer value than competitors and, hence, command a premium price (differentiation).'

Firms that operate in a number of different countries can locate processes where the best advantage lies – e.g. low labour costs, or proximity to vast markets like Japanese firms based in the UK – but at the same time, Porter argues, the most competitive ones come from home bases that are themselves strong and competitive. This sharpens up the instinct to succeed and provides valuable 'cluster' support from equally successful linked industries that act as buyers and suppliers.

This theory, developed over several books and numerous articles, reaches its full flowering in *The Competitive Advantage of Nations*, which takes as its key a 'diamond' of factors that makes some nations (and consequently their industries) more competitive than others.

The four points of this diamond are:

- *Factor conditions*: the nation's position in factors of production (such as skilled labour or infrastructure) necessary to compete in a particular industry.
- *Demand conditions*: the nature of home demand for the industry's product or service and how discriminating it is.
- *Related and supporting industries*: the presence or absence of supplier industries and related industries that are internationally competitive themselves.
- *Company strategy, structure and rivalry*: the conditions governing how firms are created, organized and managed, as well as the nature of domestic rivalry. Tough domestic rivalry breeds international success.

Firms gain competitive advantage outside their home

markets, Porter argues, when their own countries provide a dynamic competitive environment, characterized by an accumulation of specialized assets and skills and a constant stimulus to upgrade and improve their products and processes. 'Clusters' of mutually supporting industries are important to success; one reason why Britain's performance has declined over the years.

Among Porter's strategic recommendations for the competitive company are:

- Sell to the most sophisticated and demanding buyers: they will set a standard for the organization.
- Seek out buyers with the most difficult needs; they become part of a firm's R&D programme.
- Establish norms of exceeding the toughest regulatory hurdles or product standards: these provide targets that will force improvement.
- Source from the most advanced and international home-based suppliers; those with competitive advantage already will challenge the firm to improve and upgrade.
- Treat employees as permanent instead of a demoralizing hire-and-fire approach.
- Establish outstanding competitors as motivators.

One of Porter's favourite methods of identifying a firm's competitive position is to analyse its 'value chain' – all the activities it performs and how they interact. Examining these components sheds lights on the roots of costs and how they behave, and picks out existing and potential sources of differentiation. 'A firm gains competitive advantage by performing these strategically important activities more cheaply or better than its competitors.'

Kathryn Rudie Harrigan, a former student of Porter's – and now a guru in her own right as well as being professor of strategic management at New York's Columbia University – says the ideas in *Competitive Strategy* are required reading in every US business school and most executive education programmes. 'The framework he popularised forms the cornerstone for the next decade of research concerning strategy formulation . . . . The first chapter of the book he edited about global competition★ provides what has become the dominant framework for looking at issues in global strategy.'

KEY BOOKS

Porter, M. E. (1980) *Competitive Strategy: Techniques for Analysing Industries and Competitors*, New York: Free Press.
Porter, M. E. (1985) *Competitive Advantage*, New York: Free Press.
Porter, M. E. (ed) (1986) *Competition in Global Industries*, Cambridge, Mass.: Harvard Business School Press.
Porter, M. E. (1990) *The Competitive Advantage of Nations*, London: Macmillan.

★*Competition in Global Industries*, ed. by M. E. Porter (Harvard Business School Press, 1986).

27

REG REVANS

(b.1907)

Managers educating each other through 'Action Learning'

Underrated British (Southampton-born) inventor of 'Action Learning,' in which working teams of managers educate each other amid the real risk, confusion and opportunity of the workplace itself. The idea has become an accepted part of management education, though only the Japanese have fully acknowledged the importance of Revans' early work – as a foundation stone of their quality circle philosophy.

Revans, a one-time local government official working in the educational field, is known to feel bitter about his position as a guru without honour in his own country. Management consultant Bob Garratt, who worked with Revans in industry, says his theories form 'one of the few bodies of management work which are highly scientifically and mathematically based, beautifully researched.' Garratt suspects it was this that 'frightened people off,' especially in the late 1960s and early 1970s when British management education came heavily under the influence of US West Coast psychotherapy and the whole humanist, sociological approach to industry. But the theory still 'works wonderfully', says Garratt.

Revans' ideas have played an important role in management training in continental Europe. A programme in Belgium based on Revans' theories was described as being partly responsible for Belgium's 102-per-cent increase in industrial productivity between 1971 and 1981. (For comparison, Japan's figure is 85 per cent and Britain's is 28 per cent.)

In the 1970s Revans became president of the European Association of Management Training Centres, and an EC report later paid tribute to his work. (*Education in the European Community*, 1978.)

Revans said of his book *Action Learning* (1974) that he bought most of the copies as scrap. It did not sell, yet it was the culmination of some 40 years' working and thinking by Revans, who wrote his first paper on training in 1938, when he was responsible for technical and professional education on Essex County Council.

Over the next 20 years he developed the radical theory that managers learned better from each other in working management situations than they ever could in a classroom. The message was driven home for him while working in a training and development capacity in the coal-mining industry, where he observed how miners had to 'carry the educational can' in working with young newcomers to the pits. They had to combine the teaching of technical knowledge with sensitivity to the fears and insecurity of youngsters working underground for the first time.

Revans identified these abilities as essential to the manager of any large enterprise. In doing so, as one appreciation of his work puts it, he 'became a forerunner of the whole socio-technical school of management which was to blossom in the 1960s.'

From his observations in the pits, Revans concluded that miners and managers should also learn from and with each other, and he proposed the formation of a Staff College through which people in the industry with common problems could be brought together to exchange ideas for practical solutions. This was the core of Action Learning, which Revans later took into National Health Service hospitals.

Revans also studied the effect of the size of a business on the morale of people working for it, and concluded well ahead of E. F. Schumacher (a colleague of his on the Coal Board) that 'small is beautiful.'

'What does make Revans unique,' wrote Ronald Lessem of City University Business School, 'is the way he has linked together industrial relations (artisan and scribe), human relations (self and others), technological change (education and industry), and the whole question of scale (centre and periphery) with information processing, problem-solving and learning.'

Revans, said Lessem, 'placed at the centre of things the "springs of human action." It is one's perception of the problem, he said, one's evaluation of what is to be gained by solving it, and one's estimate of the resources at hand to solve it, that supply these action springs.'

Revans sees the concept as one of great antiquity, citing Buddha as 'an early believer in action learning, teaching others that it is from their own real experiences that the most fundamental truths are most likely to be learned.'

He has always taken a holistic approach, incorporating some elements of religious belief, to the practice of management. His synthesis of tasks and relationships, personal consciousness and management technique, organizational science and religious faith was distilled into *The Theory of Practice in Management* (1966). This was followed by *Developing Effective Managers* (1971), in which Revans set out a model for achieving managerial objectives, based on three systems – Alpha, Beta and Gamma. System Alpha is concerned with the manager's use of information in designing strategies; System Beta with achieving them by negotiation and System Gamma with monitoring the learning curve of adapting to experience and change.

Young, fast-track managers have responded to Action Learning more than the older generation. One of the few leading British industrialists who did recognize its practical value was Arnold (now Lord) Weinstock of GEC. Action learning has been practised in Egypt, Africa and India, and became part of many management training programmes. In February 1988 Sir Douglas Hague wrote: 'We are in a new industrial revolution which requires management trainers to develop 'action learning' from real experience within business and industry, rather than getting tied up with theory and academia.'

Revans has been quoted as saying: 'The facts now are that all I have been on about these fifty years is slowly being seen to have been right.' (*Makers of Management*, by David Clutterbuck and Stuart Crainer, 1990.) He remains convinced that action learning is an idea whose time has come – even if his own national peers should be among the last to appreciate it.

KEY BOOKS

Revans, R. W. (1966) *The Theory of Practice in Management*, London: Macdonald.
Revans, R. W. (1971) *Developing Effective Managers*,
Revans, R. W. (1979) *Action Learning*, London: Blond and Briggs.

(It is indicative of Revans' prophet-without-honour fate that a 1982 symposium of papers on his theories, published under the title *The Origins and Growth of Action Learning*, should have been published by Studentlitteratur in West Germany under the auspices of the Bratt Institut fur Neues Lernen and available in an English language version from a small Bromley firm called Chartwell-Bratt. All Revans' books are difficult to obtain outside libraries.)

28

EDGAR H. SCHEIN

The 'psychological contract' between employer and employed

American social psychologist and Professor of Management at the Sloan School of Management, Massachusetts Institute of Technology, who coined the term 'the psychological contract' to express the unwritten understandings that exist within an organization.

Schein virtually invented the concept of corporate culture – the commonly held set of assumptions about an organization's values and practices – which has only recently attracted substantial attention from management writers.

Schein worked at MIT with Douglas McGregor of 'Theory X and Theory Y' fame, and was greatly influenced by him. Britain's Charles Handy studied under Schein, Warren Bennis (qv) and Chris Argyris (qv) and has said the experience 'transformed my life.'

Edgar Schein is responsible for two coinages that have entered the language of management thinking – the 'psychological contract' and the 'career anchor.' Both are intimately connected with the analysis of motivation, which is the root of Schein's work.

The first embraces what an employee expects from those

who employ him or her, not only in economic terms like pay, conditions, hours and job security, but also how he or she is treated and encouraged to develop abilities and responsibility. Schein believes that many strikes and industrial disputes occur basically because this contract has been broken, even though the flashpoint may appear to be a specific economic grievance. The psychological contract is not one-sided; it also includes a company's expectations about the people who work for it, such as loyalty and diligence. It is essential for both aspects to match or correspond if the 'contract' is to work on a long-term basis.

Allied to this is the career anchor: the perceptions about themselves that individuals hold in a particular organization, and which encourage them to remain in that organization. These relate strongly to self-esteem and satisfaction with the way talents are allowed to develop, and tend to be moulded by experience in the early part of an organizational career.

Schein identified these as typical career anchors: how individuals viewed their technical competence, managerial competence, security and autonomy in the job they were doing. Career anchors can also, he explained, have a narrowing effect on a person's development even within an organization in which he or she seems content: for example, a graduate's view of his technical competence was such that he saw himself doing technical work only instead of expanding in mid-career into managerial responsibility.

The assumptions that individuals develop about themselves within their organization are in turn largely shaped by the assumptions those organizations hold about their own values, goals and how things are done, which they pass on in various ways to their employees.

These form a company's culture and may emerge in all kinds of ways, from the sober suits and white shirts that IBM salesmen are expected to wear to the intellectual clubbiness and sense of belonging that typify many departments within the BBC – always known simply as 'the Corporation' to its career staff. (ICI has a similar 'family' culture, and at one time its historic Mond Division, now subsumed in the restructuring of the late 1980s, had its own culture within ICI based on its leading-edge achievements in scientific innovation.)

Schein says an organization's culture is 'what it has learned as a total social unit over the course of its history.' He defines it as made up of artefacts (dress codes, office layouts, the signals a stranger would pick up); values (often enshrined in anecdotes from the founder's time) and underlying assumptions (behaviour within the organization and of the organization in the environment outside).

Consensus on such cultural landmarks among both workforce and management is essential to successful achievement of the organization's goals. Schein outlines five key areas in which this consensus should operate:

- The mission – 'what business are we in, and why?'
- The goals, which should include specific goals for all workers
- The means to accomplish the goals, including reward and incentive systems
- The means of measuring progress, including reporting and feedback
- The strategies for what to do when things go wrong

Schein's belief that the key to successful leadership is managing cultural change in an organization has made him the guru for a rapidly growing band of writers on corporate culture and how it affects, for example, the success or failure of a takeover or merger of two companies with differing cultures, or the diversification of a company into new markets. Schein designed a set of diagnostic steps to help identify such cultural and compatibility problems and suggest ways of solving them.

Diagnostic ability, indeed, is an essential attribute of good management, in Schein's view. His whole work on the roots of motivation began, like that of his mentor Douglas McGregor, by analysing the way managers view the people they manage.

Historically, these models divide into three. There is the 'rational-economic' model held by F. W. Taylor and expressed by McGregor as 'Theory X' – basically, the view that most people have to be coerced into work by economic incentives and require constant management supervision. Then there is the 'social' model, formulated by Mayo and his Hawthorne experiments, which recognized needs other than economic and the importance of a worker's peer groups on performance. The third historical concept, the 'self-actualizing' model, developed the social model further, into understanding the needs of individuals to develop their full potential. Abraham Maslow (qv) with his 'hierarchy of needs;' McGregor with Theory Y; Argyris (qv) and Herzberg (qv) were other influential gurus in this field. To these existing models, Schein added a fourth – the 'complex' model. This argued that in the huge gamut of human needs and motivations, an individual's response will be governed by many variables at different times and in different situations. Schein also examined how incentives change according to an individual's changing perceptions; for example, why millionaires and other achievers persist in seeking still more millions or in setting themselves new and more difficult goals.

Robert Browning's lines: 'A man's reach should exceed his grasp, Or what's a heaven for?' encapsulate the mystery of motivation which Edgar Schein's work sets out to unravel.

KEY BOOKS

Schein, E. H. (1978) *Career Dynamics: Matching Individual and Organizational Needs*, Wokingham: Addison-Wesley.
Schein, E. H. (1980) *Organizational Psychology*, New Jersey: Prentice-Hall.
Schein, E. H. (1985) *Organizational Culture and Leadership*, San Francisco: Jossey-Bass.

29

RICHARD J. SCHONBERGER

(b.1937)

*Each function in a business should be a
'customer' of the next in the chain*

American industrial engineer and now international consultant and lecturer, who is credited with introducing Just-
in-Time and other Japanese manufacturing techniques to
the US. After leaving college, he worked for eight years
in US defence industries – shipbuilding, aircraft overhaul,
army tank manufacturing. He then took a PhD in business
studies at the University of Nebraska, specializing in
production management and information systems, subsequently teaching there for 13 years.

At this time, he recalls, 'I was disgusted with manufacturing and thought the future lay with management
information systems. I dropped it like a hot potato when
manufacturing got exciting again.'

The catalyst in manufacturing happened through his
work with computers in industry. Material Requirements
Planning (MRP) was, he says, 'the only exciting thing to
have happened in manufacturing in 50 years.'

Schonberger's first book, *Japanese Manufacturing
Techniques* (1982), has sold over 150,000 copies in nine
languages. His second, *World Class Manufacturing* (1986)
sold 100,000 copies in eight languages, and together they
are the two best-selling books of all time on manufacturing. Each of his four books has grown out of its
predecessor, the fourth – *Building a Chain of Customers*
(1990) – developing his ultimate theory that 'world class'

excellence in manufacturing and service industries can only be achieved by regarding each function in a business as a 'customer' of the one serving it.

A workaholic lecturer who is now also consultant and trainer to many leading multinational corporations including Hewlett-Packard, IBM, 3M, Ford, Monsanto, DuPont, Philips and Zanussi, Schonberger visits at least one factory a week in the US or Europe. He claims that he never repeats an idea he has previously expounded. 'If I don't have something new to say, I'm not saying it.' Considering that he has published over 100 articles as well as three major books and two 'casebooks,' this must make him unique among management gurus.

Asked to distil his life's work into a 'mission statement,' Richard Schonberger replies: 'World class excellence is continual improvement in serving the customer's four basic wants: ever-better quality, ever-lower costs, ever-increasing flexibility and ever-quicker response. And that includes the next process in all the processes in between, all the way to the final customer.'

This is what Schonberger, the evangelist of 'customer-driven performance,' means by the title of his latest book, *Building a Chain of Customers*. In his vividly argued theories, spattered with examples and chatty miniature case studies, the many links between and within the different functions of a business – design, manufacturing, accounting, marketing – form a continuous 'chain of customers' leading directly to those who buy the final product or service. Tom Peters has called the concept 'a bold and meticulously detailed blueprint for redesigning corporations to destroy functional myopia, to live as a whole to serve the customer.'

Schonberger says of the techniques his books expound: 'They are easy to learn, don't cost much and immediately make people feel better about their jobs. Once people begin thinking that way, they cannot define their performance any other way except in the eyes of the "customer" where their work goes next.' With this simplicity, Schonberger argues that it does not take long to train existing people in industry in how to improve rapidly, 'how to love to improve and change, and become customer-focused.'

One of the major themes in his Japanese book, published in 1982, was that the Japanese success was not due to any cultural factors; that anyone could learn the techniques of Total Quality Management and so on. Studying the results as they became practised in hundreds of firms in North America between 1982 and 1986, Schonberger derived the basis of his second book, *World Class Manufacturing*. Hewlett-Packard, which sets forth its operational philosophy in a booklet called The HP Way, emerged as the best example anywhere.

Cellular manufacturing is one of Schonberger's keys to the internal customer chain. In this, clusters of people and operations are arranged according to the work flow rather than departmental requirements. He credits its invention to five British industrial pioneers between about 1965 and 1975 – Professors John L. Burbidge and G. A. B. Edwards; consultant Joseph Gombinski and works managers Gordon Ranson and Charles Allen. (Allen was manager of a Ferranti defence plant in Edinburgh that converted to the cell principle between 1968 and 1971.)

As usual, however, it was left to others to exploit and develop a brilliant British concept and to apply it to industrial practice on the shop floor.

'Toyota took those ideas, polished and perfected them and forced them on first- and second-echelon suppliers,' recalls Schonberger. 'The whole Toyota family of companies reorganised itself, moved all its machines into cells and built all its new plants according to the way the product flowed, instead of by departments.

'By and large, we owe a debt of gratitude to the Japanese for showing the power of these ideas, even though there were plenty of other people who were aware of it.'

Schonberger believes his 'customer-driven message' applies to everyone in an organization 'from the CEO to the janitor.' When lecturing for his World Class International consultancy, he often prefers to address the 'up and coming, new blood, next crop of leaders,' rather than existing top management.

'I believe the future is in the hands of the doers – the operators, assemblers, clerks, stock handlers, drivers, servers . . . The message – how to become a world-class organisation – certainly does not go over anyone's head.

'It won't be a disaster if CEOs and presidents don't read books such as mine; their lieutenants and lower-level managers, and even some of their operators do, and they will run the show right half a generation from now – if not much sooner – with or without the blessings of their high-level bosses.'

Schonberger is encouraged by the growing 'convergence' he perceives in management thinking, by how similar themes of serving the customers and involving the employees are struck in most of the recent path-setting works: he cites Tom Peters' *Thriving On Chaos*, Stanley Davis' *Future Perfect* and Grayson and O'Dell's *American Business: A Two-Minute Warning*. The voices championing the new belief in both controlling the causes of costs and focusing on the customer's primary wants (quality, throughput time, flexibility and cost) are now diverse and international, and Schonberger can claim to be among the pioneers.

KEY BOOKS

Schonberger, R. J. (1982) *Japanese Manufacturing Techniques*, New York: The Free Press.

Schonberger, R. J. (1986) *World Class Manufacturing*, New York: The Free Press.

Schonberger, R. J. (1987) *World Class Manufacturing Casebook*, New York: The Free Press.

Schonberger, R. J. (1990) *Building a Chain of Customers*, New York: The Free Press; London: Business Books.

30

E. F. SCHUMACHER

(1911–1977)

'Small is beautiful': the human scale against corporate 'giantism'

German-born economist who worked for Britain's National Coal Board for 20 years from 1950, and became famous for one idea, owed chiefly to a brilliant 'selling' title coined by his publisher. The title *Small is Beautiful* came to symbolize the whole 1970s/1980s revolt against large, impersonal organizations, yet the concept of rethinking the conduct of business, economics and government on a small, human scale was only one of a number of ideas in Schumacher's collection of essays, published in 1973 and subtitled 'A Study of Economics As If People Mattered.'

In two or three of his 19 essays Schumacher castigated what he called 'the idolatry of giantism,' whether applied to multinational business corporations, megalopolitan urban developments or the size of nations and their internal markets, and noted that the achievement of Alfred Sloan at General Motors was 'to structure this gigantic firm in such a manner that it became, in fact, a federation of fairly reasonably sized firms.'

Surprisingly, perhaps, he also cited his own organization, the National Coal Board, one of the biggest firms, albeit publicly owned, in Western Europe, as an example where 'something very similar (to Sloan's approach) was attempted under the chairmanship of Lord Robens; strenuous efforts were made to evolve a structure which would maintain the unity of one big organisation and at the same time create the 'climate' or feeling of there being a federation of numerous 'quasi-firms'. The monolith was transformed into a well co-ordinated assembly of lively, semi-autonomous units, each with its own drive and sense of achievement.

'While many theoreticians – who may not be too closely in touch with real life – are still engaging in the idolatry of large size, with practical people in the actual world there is a tremendous longing and striving to profit, if at all possible, from the convenience, humanity and manageability of smallness.'

Schumacher's prescriptions did not go much beyond such broad-brush statements (indeed, elsewhere in his book he argues quite passionately for the virtues of nationalized industry, not usually associated with the 'small is beautiful' movement), yet his approach – philosophical, influenced by eastern religions such as Buddhism, and linked to the fulfilment and happiness of human beings in their working and social contexts – struck a resonant chord that reverberated long after the contents of his modest essays were forgotten. He was ahead of his time by about 15 years in advising the recognition of people's need to be involved in decision-making in small units: in the late 1980s Rosabeth Moss Kanter and other gurus would call it 'empowerment' and write whole books about it. Charles Handy says Schumacher has been 'enormously influential in spite of himself,' but today it seems incredible that so much fame could have been built on such slender foundations. Even President Jimmy Carter is said to have read and been influenced by Schumacher's book.

As well as his work for the Coal Board, Schumacher set up the International Technology Development Group and became an adviser on economic problems to Third World countries. He always advocated small-scale production techniques and said 'organisations should imitate nature, which doesn't allow a single cell to become too large.'

KEY BOOK

Schumacher, E. F. (1973) *Small is Beautiful*, London: Blond & Briggs.

31

ALFRED P. SLOAN

(1875–1966)

*Developed the key principle of decentralization
for big corporations*

US industrialist, head of General Motors from the early
1920s to the mid-1950s, and the man who virtually
invented the decentralized, multi-divisional corporation
of today. Sloan's name crops up more often in the indexes
of management books than that of any other individual
in industry – Peter Drucker's magisterial *Management:
Tasks, Responsibilities, Practices* has over 25 page references to him.

Sloan wrote only one book, and that with assistance
from a professional editor on *Fortune*; not usually enough
to justify guru status in the management world, but that
book, *My Years With General Motors* (1963), has been
immensely influential on practising managers and on the
study of organizations. James O'Toole, professor of
management at the University of Southern California,
called it 'the model for how managers should think –
indeed, the model for much management education.' Sir
John Egan, when he was chairman of Jaguar Cars, wrote
in the preface to a new edition: 'I believe that this book
should be on the reading list of everyone who can
influence, or is influenced by, industrial enterprise.'

What was remarkable about Sloan's achievement in
reorganizing the moribund General Motors of 1921 into
America's leading automobile company within three
years was not only that his innovations succeeded so

quickly but that they have stood the test of decades of change and are still models of organizational thinking in a business world unrecognizable from that of 1921.

Twenty-five years after Sloan restructured GM, Henry Ford's grandson applied the same principles at Ford and within five years had regained the company's growth and profit potential. Nearly 30 years after Sloan's revolution, in the early 1950s, General Electric adapted his design and it became, in Peter Drucker's words, 'the standard model worldwide.'

An electrical engineer by training and a graduate of MIT (he later helped finance its Sloan School of Management), Sloan was the general manager of the Hyatt Roller Bearing Company in 1900, when it merged with United Motors. In 1917, United was acquired by General Motors and Sloan, by then United's president, joined the GM board. He became president in 1923, chairman in 1946 and honorary chairman from 1956 until his death ten years later.

Sloan's celebrated design for 'federal decentralization' – autonomous divisions subject to financial and policy controls from a small corporate staff – took him only one month to construct, working with a small committee of top GM executives. Pierre S. Du Pont, head of the chemical company which was a major shareholder in GM, had asked him to help pull GM back from the brink of bankruptcy, and Du Pont himself had earlier restructured his company along decentralized lines between 1915 and 1920; a fact which has led some management writers to assume that Sloan simply borrowed the idea.

In fact, the two firms had been suffering from opposing problems – Du Pont being heavily over-centralized, while GM was already untidily decentralized without adequate central control. In working out his own solution, Sloan greatly refined and polished the decentralization principle and, most importantly, developed the first systematic approaches to strategic planning. GM became the first company to change completely, through a planned strategy, the accepted manufacturing and marketing methods of an industry.

Such was the impact of this new approach that within ten years of the outbreak of World War I, the number of US automobile companies fell from over 100 to around a dozen, of which three (Ford, GM and Chrysler) accounted for fully 90 per cent of sales.

Alfred Pritchard Sloan, the Brooklyn-accented son of a New York tea, coffee and cigar wholesaler, was put in charge of General Motors in the midst of the worst slump to hit the infant automobile industry. William S. Durant had put together GM out of eight independent companies, all still run as virtual baronies by their owners, and it was plagued by over-production and wasteful duplication. Ford had 60 per cent of the US market with a single model – the Model T, cheap, standardized and black. General Motors had 12 per cent of the market with eight models, only two of which made a profit.

Sloan's 'federal' plan was designed to do more than rationalize GM's messy structure with centralized financial and policy control and professionally managed divisions each responsible for its own performance. It was to be the mechanism by which he could define and implement a new mission for GM – to produce a car for 'every purse and purpose.'

Up to that time the US auto industry was producing to just two levels of customer demand, the mass market and the class market; i.e. high-volume, low-priced cars, dominated by the Model T, and low-volume, high-priced cars. Sloan perceived much more varied and aspirational possibilities. He devised a five-model range, each overlapping in price and performance with the next, so that the low-income customer could pay a little more than for the Model T and get a car with far better styling and performance (and in other colours than black). At the same time, better-off purchasers could choose to economize with a good-looking low-priced car or pay slightly more and get a near-luxury model. Each of the five cars was designed to be a market leader in its class and competed with the GM car on either side of it, whether Chevrolet, Oldsmobile, Pontiac, Buick or Cadillac.

Sloan also introduced optional extras to stimulate customer interest, and by bringing in a new model every year he virtually invented the used-car market. This killed the changeless, all-alike Model T more quickly than any direct competition could have done. The one-year-old GM car, more stylish and a better performer than the Ford, could now beat it even on price.

The new organization Sloan devised reduced GM's eight car companies into five operating divisions, buttressed by three component divisions. Each division had its own engineering, production and sales departments but was supervised by a central corporate staff responsible for policy and finance. In every other way, each division was truly a business, with its chief executive responsible to Sloan as vice-president. (Sloan also introduced the innovation of taking a lower salary than the high-flyers who reported to him, the career professional). GM's accessory divisions sold both to the car divisions and to outside customers, including GM's competitors. This was a principle which retained its value as recently as Sir John Harvey-Jones's reorganization of ICI on a business-unit basis.

Sloan's ideas, in fact, were very largely based on the functional analysis of management drawn up by Henri Fayol in the previous century. Where Fayol had achieved the organizational solution for the single-product manufacturing business, Sloan accomplished it for the large, complex manufacturing business of the mass-production age.

Sloan introduced a system of checks and balances into the divisional structure that gave engineering, manufacturing and finance equal status. In time, however, his network of committees and policy groups, designed to produce impartial and even-handed decisions, became riddled with factions and the financial arm prevailed. Over-production ensued and GM's market share in the 1980s dropped by 15 per cent. Sloan's design has now had a rebuild, but it had served GM well for nearly 60 years.

Sloan was a firm believer in the impersonal, task-focused

concept of management. He was also an early believer in encouraging the sort of creative dissent that Tom Peters (qv) and Richard Pascale (qv) are recommending for keeping companies vigorous and innovative in the 1990s. Peter Drucker and other management writers like to quote a story about Sloan chairing a meeting of one of GM's top committees. At the end of the discussion, he said: 'Gentlemen, I take it we are all in complete agreement on the decision here.' Everyone round the table nodded. 'Then,' said Sloan, 'I propose we postpone further discussion of this matter until the next meeting to give ourselves time to develop disagreement, and perhaps gain some understanding of what the decision is all about.'

Sloan was almost alone among practising managers before World War II to evolve management theories that have become classics. The other well-known example is Chester Barnard of American Telephone. But Sloan's achievements, though renowned throughout the automobile industry, only became widely known in 1963 when he published *My Years With General Motors*. The book became one of the first best-selling management biographies.

By this time, however, Sloan was nearly 90 and the book, it must be said, is no racy read along the lines of an Iacocca or Geneen. It is formal, old-fashioned and sometimes pedantic in style; nevertheless it provides a matchlessly detailed and authentic picture of how US industry was run between the wars. No one else could have produced so authoritative a case study as this man who, born in 1875, had grown up with the automobile and very largely shaped its place in modern American life.

The essentials of Sloan's organizational genius, however, can be more clearly picked out in books by others – Drucker's *Managing for Results*, for example, or his *Concept of the Corporation*. *My Years With General Motors* is best read as a slice of nutritious if sometimes dry industrial and social history.

KEY BOOK

Sloan, A. P. (1963, 1966, 1986) *My Years With General Motors*, New York: Doubleday; London: Sidgwick and Jackson; Penguin Books.

32

F. W. TAYLOR

(1856–1917)

The science of work and 'functional management'

Frederick Winslow Taylor was the American Quaker engineer who invented scientific management, the forerunner of time and motion study and work study. He spent his industrial career in steel companies, starting as a labourer with the Midvale Steel Works, where he ended as chief engineer, and then moving to the Bethlehem Steel Works of Pittsburgh as a consulting engineer in management. It was here that he carried out his celebrated experiments in breaking down the components of a manual task like shifting pig-iron, timing each movement with a stop-watch. He believed there could be a proven best way to perform each task in a factory, that every employee could be trained to be 'first-class' at some job, and that it was management's responsibility to identify these possibilities and provide opportunities for improvement.

Even at college, where he was nicknamed 'Speedy,' Taylor was obsessed with improving efficiency: he succeeded in getting the rules of baseball changed by proving that over-arm bowling was more effective than under-arm. (He was less successful in persuading the tennis authorities that a spoon-shaped racket was more efficient than an oval one.)

His ground-breaking book, *Principles of Scientific Management*, developed out of several academic papers, was published in 1911. A British army officer named Major Lyndall Urwick, reading Taylor in the trenches of the First World War, was inspired to found a movement for scientific management in Britain: he later became Britain's first professional management consultant. In the US, Taylor's work was carried forward and developed by the time-and-motion study experts Frank and Lillian Gilbreth and other industrial psychologists.

Frederick W. Taylor believed in one maxim above all, that 'the principal object of management should be to secure the maximum prosperity for the employer, coupled with the maximum prosperity of each employee.' To this end he preached that management and workforce were interdependent and relied on each other to achieve the common goal of higher prosperity. An early experiment as consultant to a ball-bearing company on raising the quality of their product was conducted on the principle of a modern quality circle, with the workers becoming responsible for their own improvement.

'Under scientific management,' Taylor wrote, 'the initiative of the workmen – that is, their hard work, their good will, their ingenuity – is obtained practically with absolute regularity, while under even the best of the older type of management the initiative is only obtained spasmodically and somewhat irregularly . . . By far the greater gain under scientific management comes from the new, the very great and the extraordinary burdens and duties which are voluntarily assumed by those on the management's side.'★

Principles of Scientific Management rested on four 'great underlying principles of management.' These were:

1. The development of a science of work to replace the old

★F. W. Taylor (1947) *Scientific Management*, New York: Harper and Row, quoted in *Organization Theory*, (1990) ed. D. S. Pugh London: Penguin Books.

rule-of-thumb methods by which workmen operated. Fulfilling optimum goals would earn higher wages; failure to do so would result in loss of earnings.
2. Scientific selection and progressive development of the worker: training each to be 'first-class' at some task.
3. Bringing together the science of work and the scientifically selected and trained workers for best results.
4. Equal division of work and responsibility between workers and management, cooperating together in close interdependence.

In Taylor's thinking, every task, whether of worker or manager, became discrete and specialized. In its application to management, he described this as 'functional management.' On the worker's side, he saw benefits of increased earnings, by between 30 and 100 per cent.

Although Taylor's theories of industrial engineering are now largely discredited – the US labour unions never accepted them – they have resilient powers of survival. Robert Waterman, the co-author of *In Search of Excellence* and author of *The Renewal Factor*, says many managers of the 90s continue to practise Taylorism without realizing it.

And, as Peter Drucker acknowledged in *Management: Tasks, Responsibilities, Practices*, Taylor was 'the first man in history who did not take work for granted, but looked at it and studied it.'

KEY BOOK

Taylor, F. W. (1947) *Scientific Management*, New York: Harper and Row.

33

MAX WEBER

(1864–1920)

How individuals respond to authority in organizations

German sociologist and political economist, trained as a lawyer, who taught at Berlin University and later became professor of economics at the universities of Freiburg, Heidelberg and Munich. In 1918 he was a member of the committee set up to draft the constitution of the Weimar Republic. His widest-read book was – and remains – *The Protestant Ethic and the Spirit of Capitalism*, a short and stimulating thesis that linked the moral imperatives of puritanical Protestantism, especially Calvinism, with the mainspring of entrepreneurial capitalism, the pursuit of profit and, ultimately, with the 'iron cage' of modern materialism. Weber's chief interest to students of management and organization theory – though now much less influential than it used to be – lies in *The Theory of Social and Economic Organisation*, first published in 1924, four years after his death.

Max Weber was the first writer on management theory to analyse the role of the leader in an organization and to examine how and why individuals respond to various forms of authority. He was probably the first, since the Greeks coined the term, to use 'charisma' in its modern sense of that quality in an individual's personality which effortlessly draws others to follow.

Weber distinguished three types of legitimate authority, as opposed to power, which forces people to obey: the rational, the traditional and the charismatic. The rational, or rational-legal, which he saw as the dominant form of modern institution, rested on a system of rationally thought-out goals and functions designed to maximize the performance of an organization and implemented by certain rules and procedures. Authority here was vested in the office of a person rather than in the individual. It was an impersonal system which he described, with no criticism implied, as a bureaucracy. He held a bureaucracy to be the most efficient form of administration because it worked on a commonly accepted hierarchical basis without personal whim and with a judicious reliance on the appointment of experts.

The traditional form of authority in organizations was seen by Weber as being owed to the person rather than the office; typically, a hereditary system where the leader's writ is established by precedent, as in a family business. It has roots in feudal rights and duties but is not unknown in modern firms where patronage may take the place of inheritance. Weber's concept of tradition may also be detected in the cultures of those companies where the attitude 'we've always done it this way' becomes a self-justification resistant to critical analysis by newcomers.

Charismatic authority, because it relies on the particular qualities of an individual, is unlikely to find a successor in its own mould. Organizations with charismatic founders like Henry Ford or Thomas J. Watson of IBM tend to mutate, either into the traditional (hereditary) mode, with greater or lesser success, or into a succession determined by impersonal factors and hence into a rational, bureaucratic form.

Weber was in no doubt that the latter system was the buttress of efficient administration in whatever kind of institution it operates. 'Precision, speed, unambiguity, knowledge of files, continuity, discretion, unity, strict subordination, reduction of friction and of material and personal costs – these are raised to the optimum point in the strictly bureaucratic administration,' he wrote.

The system's machine-like superiority over other types of authority rests on its hierarchical form, with each office subordinate to the one above it; every official's role determined by written rules; a regulated right of appeal and the ability to take grievances upwards; and complete separation of the administrative staff from ownership of the means of production or administration, as well as a complete absence of 'rights' to any office by its incumbent.

The purest type of bureaucratic administration, says Weber, exists when its officials conduct the business according to ten criteria:

1. They are personally free, subject only to authority in respect of their impersonal official obligations.
2. They are organized in a clearly defined hierarchy of offices.
3. Each office has a clearly defined sphere of competence in the legal sense.
4. The office is filled by a free, contractual relationship. Thus, in principle, there is free selection.
5. Candidates are selected on the basis of technical qualifications. In the most rational case, this is tested by examination or guaranteed by diplomas certifying technical training, or both. They are appointed, not elected.
6. They are remunerated by fixed salaries in money, for the most part with a right to pensions. Only under certain circumstances does the employing authority, especially in private organizations, have a right to terminate the appointment, but the official is always free to resign. The salary scale is primarily graded according to rank in the hierarchy; but in addition to this criterion, the responsibility of the position and the requirements of the incumbent's social status may be taken into account.
7. The office is treated as the sole, or at least the primary, occupation of the incumbent.
8. It constitutes a career. There is a system of 'promotion'

according to seniority or to achievement, or to both. Promotion is dependent on the judgment of superiors.
9. The official works entirely separated from ownership of the means of administration, and without appropriation of his position.
10. He is subject to strict and systematic discipline and control in the conduct of the office.*

Weber's ten criteria are in the process of being dismantled in much contemporary management thinking, such as the work of Charles Handy and Rosabeth Moss Kanter, who anticipate a sea-change in both the hierarchical nature of organizations and the concept of life-long bureaucratic careers. But a century ago, Weber was utterly convinced of the superiority of this form of harnessing the corporate effort of individuals, and many an organization in the 1990s testifies to its durability:

'Experience tends universally to show that the purely bureaucratic type of administrative organization – that is, the monocratic variety of bureaucracy – is, from a purely technical point of view, capable of attaining the highest degree of efficiency and is in this sense formally the most rational known means of carrying out imperative control over human beings. It is superior to any other form in precision, in stability, in the stringency of its discipline, and in its reliability. It thus makes possible a particularly high degree of calculability of results for the heads of the organization and for those acting in relation to it. It is finally superior both in intensive efficiency and in the scope of its operations, and is formally capable of application to all kinds of administrative tasks.'*

*Taken from *The Theory of Social and Economic Organisation*, translated and edited by A. M. Henderson and T. Parsons. New York: Free Press. Quoted in *Organization Theory* (1990) edited by D. S. Pugh, London: Penguin Books.

KEY BOOKS

Weber, M. (1930) *The Protestant Ethic and the Spirit of Capitalism*, London: Allen and Unwin.
Weber, M. (1947) *The Theory of Social and Economic Organisation*, New York: The Free Press.

GLOSSARY OF
MANAGEMENT TERMS

Action learning
A system of management education, invented by the British guru Reg Revans, in which a group of working managers learn by discussing each other's practical problems.

Adhocracy
The opposite of bureaucracy: a term originally coined by Warren Bennis and subsequently adopted by Alvin Toffler, Henry Mintzberg and Robert Waterman to describe small, flexible project teams or groups that operate freely across the departmental boundaries of an organization.

Career anchor
Term coined by Edgar Schein to denote the perceptions that individuals hold about themselves in their jobs – and which encourage them to stay in those jobs.

Champions
Influential individuals, often in research-based companies, whose backing can ensure that a project or invention gets the chance to prove itself. Peters and Waterman's *In Search of Excellence* found that companies which nurtured champions were more likely to qualify as excellent.

167

Competitive advantage

The factor that enables a company to gain an edge on its rivals in the marketplace, the result of **competitive strategy**. Harvard's Michael Porter has worked out a sophisticated formula for determining how companies – and countries – can gain competitive advantage.

Decentralization

The principle (first recognized in management writing by Alfred D. Chandler but put into practice decades before, in the early 1920s, by Alfred P. Sloan at General Motors) of devolving substantial amounts of managerial power and accountability away from the centre of a large and diverse corporation to semi-autonomous divisions or business units. After Sloan's book was published in 1963, decentralization became the vogue among large industrial conglomerates.

Empowerment

The fashionable managerial buzzword of the early 1990s. In organizations it is usually taken to mean increased participation by employees in the enterprise for which they work, with a view to stimulating initiative and entrepreneurism. It has particular implications for women in eroding the invisible barriers that tend to keep them in mundane organizational roles. Rosabeth Moss Kanter is the leading exponent of empowerment as an aid to releasing forces for innovation and change within a corporation.

Hierarchy of needs

Motivation model constructed by Abraham Maslow which charts the progression of human needs in the workplace from basic urges of warmth, food and safety to love, esteem and personal fulfilment. Maslow teaches that none of the wants is absolute: that, indeed, a satisfied want ceases to be important.

Job enrichment

Enhancing work by motivational factors that meet employees' aspirations in (usually) non-monetary ways. Frederick Herzberg, who coined the concept, said wryly that it had 'given employment to a hell of a lot of consultants'.

Just-in-time
Revolutionary Japanese low-inventory system for speeding up production, keeping it flexible to customers' requirements and cutting costs. Suppliers supply what is needed *when* it is needed, resulting in faster responses to the market.

Lateral thinking
Defined by the Oxford English Dictionary as 'seeking to solve problems by unorthodox or apparently illogical methods'. Inventor Edward de Bono, who has applied the principle to dozens of challenging situations, including management, describes its purpose as 'the generation of new ideas and the escape from old ones'.

Management by objectives
In its heyday in the 1970s, MBO divides corporate goals into objectives that can be assigned to individual managers and measured against performance. Like many other seminal ideas, MBO originated in the fertile mind of Peter Drucker, but was enlarged and developed into a practical method- ology in the late 1960s and early 1970s by the British management consultant John Humble.

Managerial hierarchies
The analysis of bureaucratic administration, with each office subordinate to the one above it and every official's role determined by his office, was first undertaken by Max Weber. Alfred Chandler carried it further in his studies of the executive function in great US corporations, arguing that the way an organization's hierarchy operates is determined by its strategic goals. Many of today's gurus, led by Rosabeth Moss Kanter, Charles Handy and the indestructible Peter Drucker, predict that the future will see flatter, non-hierarchical management structures in which the 'boss' principle is less important than empowering a wide range of contributory talents.

Mission statement
The distillation of a company's philosophy and corporate goals and values. It can range in length from a sentence to

a book (viz. the IBM classic, *A Business and Its Beliefs*, by Thomas J. Watson, Jr., son of the firm's founder).

Motivational theories

Management theory underwent a sea-change in the 1930s when scientific management, emphasizing measurement of task and performance, gave way to social psychology and human relations, emphasizing the role and motivation of the individual. Elton Mayo, in his seminal work at Western Electric's Hawthorne plant in Chicago in the late 1920s and early 1930s, was the first to identify psychological elements leading to increased productivity. Later theories have included the hierarchy of needs (qv) and the psychological contract (qv), but all have stressed the importance of the peer group in job satisfaction and self-esteem.

Portfolio work

Charles Handy's attractive view of the future for many 'knowledge workers', who, as long-term careers in one organization become rarer, will increasingly divide their time into two, three or more discretionary areas of work. Some may be voluntary (e.g. part-time clergy) or otherwise unpaid (e.g. mature student), but have the potential to enhance the quality of the individual's life and personal development.

Psychological contract

Term coined by Edgar Schein to denote what an employee may expect from his or her employer – less in material rewards than in the opportunities to realize potential. It applies also to the employer's expectations of those who work for an organization.

Quality management

How production faults can be eliminated by a management-led philosophy of continuous improvement in every process of planning, production and service. W. Edwards Deming laid down the principle that all processes are vulnerable to loss of quality through variations but that the levels of variation can be managed in order to raise quality consistency. Both Deming and fellow quality guru Joseph Juran insist that quality control starts at the top: Deming believes that 85 per cent of production faults are the responsibility of management.

Seven 'S' model
The system devised by the then McKinsey team of Richard Pascale, Tom Peters and Robert Waterman to measure the quality of a company's performance: the seven 'S' factors divide into three 'hard' – strategy, structure and systems – and four 'soft' – style, shared values, skills and staff. Pascale used the model in *The Art of Japanese Management* in case studies comparing US and Japanese companies; Peters and Waterman employed it for *In Search of Excellence*.

Theory X and Theory Y
The terms coined by Douglas McGregor to epitomize two diametrically opposed sets of management assumptions whose roots go back to Aristotle and Plato. Theory X assumes that most human beings are lazy, dislike work and responsibility and need to be firmly directed; Theory Y that they actively want to work, achieve and assume responsibility, and should be allowed more self-direction. Before his death in 1964 McGregor was evolving a refined 'Theory Z', but this term was later adopted and adapted by William Ouchi in his book of that title.

Vertical integration
The system favoured by some large corporations for integrating a number of companies down to supplier level to act as an in-house chain of manufacture. Once an established and successful strategy of the US automobile industry, its weaknesses are now more clearly seen as companies have learned that they can't be equally good at a variety of activities. 'Partnering' suppliers rather than integrating them is now the vogue.

RECOMMENDED GENERAL READING

Pugh, D.S. and Hickson, D.J. eds (1990, 4th edition): *Writers on Organizations*, London, Penguin.

Key readings from the works of gurus who have contributed to the study or organizations, including 17 of the thinkers in Guide to the Management Gurus.

Pugh, D.S. ed (1990, 3rd edition): *Organization Theory: Selected Readings,* London, Penguin.

Helpfully chosen tastings from important writings including McGregor's Theory X and Y, Mayo on the Hawthorne experiments and key articles by Mintzberg and R.M. Kanter.

Clutterbuck, David and Crainer, Stuart (1990) *Makers of Management,* London, Macmillan.

Stimulating history of management ideas and the people who evolved them, both academics and industrialists, with a useful chronology of management thinking and an excellent bibliography.